INTERACTIVE MODELS FOR OPERATIONS AND SUPPLY CHAIN MANAGEMENT

The McGraw-Hill/Irwin Series

Operations and Decision Sciences

INTERACTIVE MODELS FOR OPERATIONS AND SUPPLY CHAIN MANAGEMENT

Byron J. Finch

Miami University
Oxford, Ohio

McGraw-Hill Irwin

Boston   Burr Ridge, IL   Dubuque, IA   Madison, WI   New York   San Francisco   St. Louis
Bangkok   Bogotá   Caracas   Kuala Lumpur   Lisbon   London   Madrid   Mexico City
Milan   Montreal   New Delhi   Santiago   Seoul   Singapore   Sydney   Taipei   Toronto

INTERACTIVE MODELS FOR OPERATIONS AND SUPPLY CHAIN MANAGEMENT

Published by McGraw-Hill/Irwin, a business unit of The McGraw-Hill Companies, Inc., 1221 Avenue of the Americas, New York, NY, 10020.

Some ancillaries, including electronic and print components, may not be available to customers outside the United States.

This book is printed on acid-free paper.

1 2 3 4 5 6 7 8 9 0 QPD/QPD 0 9 8 7 6 5

ISBN-13:   978-0-07-285710-8
ISBN-10:   0-07-285710-2

Editorial director: *Stewart Mattson*
Executive editor: *Scott Isenberg*
Developmental editor: *Cynthia Douglas*
Senior marketing manager: *Douglas Reiner*
Senior media producer: *Victor Chiu*
Project manager: *Gina F. DiMartino*
Senior production supervisor: *Rose Hepburn*
Senior designer: *Adam Rooke*
Cover design: *Jillian Lindner*
Typeface: *10/13 TimesNewRomanPS*
Compositor: *Interactive Composition Corporation*
Printer: *Quebecor World Dubuque, Inc.*

Library of Congress Cataloging-in-Publication Data

Finch, Byron J.
  Interactive models for operations and supply chain management / Byron J. Finch.—1st ed.
    p. cm.—(The McGraw-Hill/Irwin series operations and decision sciences)
  ISBN-13: 978-0-07-285710-8
  ISBN-10: 0-07-285710-2 (alk. paper)
    1. Business logistics—Management. 2. Production management. 3. Industrial management. I. Title: Operations and supply chain management. II. Title. III. Series.
  HD38.5.F56 2007
  658.5—dc22

                                                                    2005052275

www.mhhe.com

Preface

Interactive Models for Operations and Supply Chain Management is designed to provide operations management and supply chain management faculty with hands-on tools that will enhance their students' understanding of critical concepts beyond what can be accomplished by simply solving problems. The 24 models provided are Java applets that allow students to manipulate parameters of a variety of models, from quantitative models such as breakeven analysis and exponential smoothing, to more sophisticated tabular techniques such as aggregate planning, risk pooling, and material requirements planning. In addition to the static models that allow user input and what-if analysis, simulation-oriented models for waiting lines, production lines, and the bullwhip effect are provided as well.

Each of the models provides a rich pedagogical tool for classroom demonstration of the interaction among variables in the models. In addition to the flexibility each model offers for close examination of a concept, each model also accompanies an interactive case that the startup default values in the model support. For each case, the function of the model is described, the case scenario is presented, and a structured guide to the case analysis is provided to ensure that students' experimentation with the model is constructive and that when analysis is complete, they have a thorough understanding of the interactions among the critical variables and parameters.

Acknowledgments

The development of *Interactive Models for Operations and Supply Chain Management* was motivated by faculty who praised the initial interactive models created for *Operations Now,* an introductory operations management text I authored for McGraw-Hill. Through the support of Scott Isenberg, my editor on that project, additional models were designed and then coded to provide a stand-alone product so that users of other texts could enjoy the benefits of this technology. I would like to thank Scott for his support of the concept of these models and for recognizing the need to accompany them with pedagogy that will expand their use. I would also like to thank Bill Sun and his team at Accelet Corporation. Accelet's ability to take my logic and interface ideas and translate them into Java applets in a very short period of time made the project enjoyable and the final models outstanding.

About the Author

Byron J. Finch is a professor of Operations Management in the Richard T. Farmer School of Business Administration at Miami University, in Oxford, Ohio. He earned his BS and MS degrees from Iowa State University and received his doctorate from the William Terry College of Business Administration at the University of Georgia in 1986. In 1987, he began teaching and research responsibilities at Miami University, where he has taught operations management courses at the undergraduate and graduate levels.

Dr. Finch's research interests have evolved from the topic of manufacturing planning and control systems early in his career, to spreadsheet models, to his most recent research endeavors that involve the use of Internet-based conversations as information to improve quality and quality expectations in the anonymous environments of online auction. As the U.S. economy has shifted toward services, Dr. Finch's research interests have become more inclusive of services as well, particularly online services. Research projects that Dr. Finch has been involved with have resulted in numerous publications in such outlets as the *Journal of Operations Management,* the *International Journal of Production Research, Quality Management Journal, Academy of Management Journal, Production and Inventory Management Journal,* and the *International Journal of Quality and Reliability Management.* Dr. Finch has also authored and co-authored other books including *The Management Guide to Internet Resources* (1997), *Operations Management: Competing in a Changing Environment* (1995), *Spreadsheet Applications for Production and Operations Management* (1990), and *Planning and Control System Design: Principles and Cases for Process Manufacturers* (1987). In addition to the traditional print publications, Dr. Finch has been the managing editor for the Operations Management Center Web site (http://www.mhhe.com/pom/) since 1998. Dr. Finch serves on the editorial boards of the *Journal of Operations Management* and the *Quality Management Journal.*

Dr. Finch has been actively involved in teaching innovation since beginning his academic career in 1986. He received the Southern Business Administration Innovative Teaching Award in 1987, the NCR Computer Innovation Award in 1990, and the Richard T. Farmer School of Business Teaching Award in 1996. Dr. Finch was nominated for the Miami University Associated Student Government Teaching Award in 2002.

Dr. Finch has held various offices in the Midwest Decision Sciences Institute, including president. He has also been involved in the Decision Sciences Institute at the national level, including a term as regionally elected vice president. Dr. Finch is also a member of the Production and Operations Management Society (POMS).

Table of Contents

Unit 1

Demand Forecasting

Models in This Unit:

The Time Series Components Model

The Simple Exponential Smoothing Model

The Trend Enhanced Exponential Smoothing Model

The Linear Trend Equation Model

The Simple Linear Regression Model

Unit 1 contains five interactive models related to forecasting. The first, the **Time Series Components Model,** provides a conceptual view of how the time series components of seasonality, trend, and random fluctuation can interact.

The remaining four models offer detailed experimentation and analysis of four popular forecasting techniques. The **Simple Exponential Smoothing Model** allows the user to vary the smoothing constant and graphically observe the change in the forecasts and accuracy measures. The **Trend Enhanced Exponential Smoothing Model** allows the user to manipulate both smoothing constants and observe the change in the forecast and accuracy measures. The **Linear Trend Equation Model** allows the user to manipulate demand data points and interpret the impact on the trend line. The **Simple Linear Regression Model** allows the user manipulation similar to that of the Linear Trend Equation Model.

The Time Series Components Model

The components of a time series include random fluctuation, seasonality, trend, and cycle. In most cases involving product demand, a cycle component is not visible because of the short time frame of the data. Different types of forecasting techniques are used, depending on the components present in the time series of interest. Understanding how these components can relate and affect each other is important if time series forecasting techniques are to be fully understood.

The Time Series Components Model provides a conceptual view of the interaction among the three dominant components of a time series: random fluctuation, seasonality, and trend. System inputs consist of a slider for each component, allowing the user to increase or decrease each to explore how various combinations affect the appearance of the time series.

Exhibit 1.1 shows the Time Series Components Model.

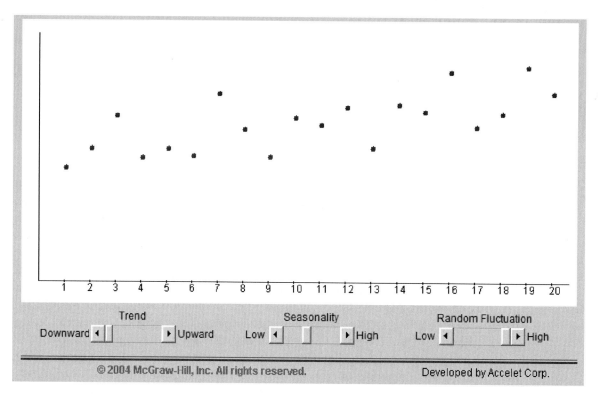

Developed by Accelet Corp.

EXHIBIT 1.1   Screen View of the Time Series Components Model

Interactive Case

Finding Seasonality at Mitchell Tax Service

For years, Mitchell Tax Service has been challenged by training the correct number of tax analysts to meet the demand for its services. It pays competitive salaries and is usually able to find high-quality employees, but seems either to train too many people, resulting in excess capacity, or not train enough people, resulting in long delays for customers. Matt Dvorak, the chief operating officer, has been badgered by his boss because of the staffing problems. Matt has concluded that improving the accuracy of the firm's demand forecast would result in a better match between capacity and demand, better service for customers, and increased profitability. Matt has examined the past demand and, from its appearance, has concluded that there is a slight upward trend and lots of random fluctuation. Being in the tax preparation business, Matt also suspects that the demand is seasonal, corresponding to the periods immediately before quarterly payments are due and to April 15. The data, however, do not seem to show a definite seasonal pattern.

Analysis

1. Examine the graph of the time series with the adjustment slides set to their default values (trend: far left; seasonality: two "clicks" from the far left; random fluctuation: far right).

    a. Describe the trend, seasonality, and random fluctuation visible in the time series. Do you agree with Matt that seasonality appears to be absent in the graph? Does the absence of a visible seasonal pattern necessarily mean that there is no seasonality?

    b. Slowly move the trend slide completely to the right and then back all the way to the left. Explain what happens to the graph. Does the visibility of random fluctuation and seasonality change?

2. Move the trend slide back to its original position at the far left end. Slowly move the random fluctuation slide to the left, one "click" at a time.

    a. Explain what happens to the graph as the amount of random fluctuation in the time series is reduced.

    b. Leave the random fluctuation slide to the far left. This has effectively eliminated the random fluctuation in the time series. What remains in the time series? Move the trend slide to the center position. What does this do to the time series? With the random fluctuation eliminated, and the trend "flat," what causes the variability of the demand data?

    c. Explain what has been happening to Matt's data that has made it impossible for him to see seasonality.

    d. Because Matt does not have an interactive model like this one, what would you suggest he do to get a better understanding of the components of his data?

The Simple Exponential Smoothing Model

Simple exponential smoothing is a popular forecasting technique, particularly when trying to smooth out the effects of random fluctuation. Simple exponential smoothing is actually a sophisticated weighted average technique that allows the user to specify the relative weight given the immediate past demand and the demands from the more distant past. The greater the weight on past demands, and the less the weight on the most recent demand, the less the impact of recent changes on the forecast. The lower the weight on the most recent demand, the greater the smoothing effect, and the less the forecast responds to demand changes. The responsiveness of the forecast is controlled by the size of α (alpha). A larger α results in a greater weight being placed on the most recent demand and less on the previous forecasts.

Exhibit 1.2 shows the Simple Exponential Smoothing Model.

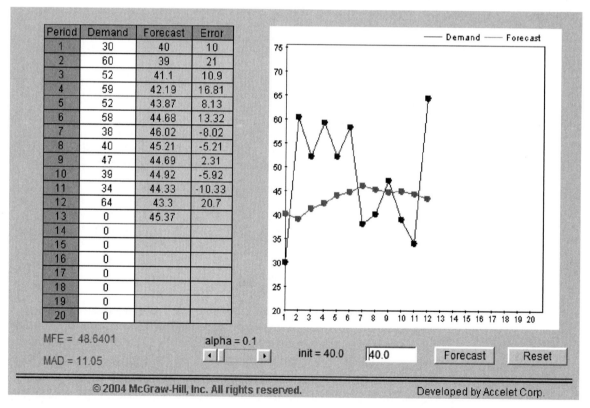

EXHIBIT 1.2   Screen View of the Simple Exponential Smoothing Model

Interactive Case

Reducing Coffee Waste by Forecasting Accurately

A local branch office of a large consulting firm has gourmet coffee delivered twice a day from a local coffee shop. Coffee is delivered in large urns at 7:30 a.m. and again at noon. Connie Andrews, the office manager, wants to continue to provide the service as a "perk" to the employees, but she does not want to pay for coffee that is ultimately thrown away. Analysis of the coffee demand shows that over the long term there appears to be no seasonal pattern or trend. In the short term, however, there are often periods of time when demand seems to be increasing, and then it shifts and decreases for a period of weeks. The most recent 12 weeks of demand are presented below.

Period	1	2	3	4	5	6	7	8	9	10	11	12
Demand	30	60	52	59	52	58	38	40	47	39	34	64

Analysis

1. Make sure that the starting default values match the demands provided above. Examine the graph of the demand for coffee. Examine how the forecast follows the demand when the alpha value is set to 0.1.

   a. Change the alpha value to 0.3. What happens to the forecast? Pay particular attention to the impact that the demand increase in period 2 and the demand decrease in period 7 have on the subsequent forecasts. What happens to the "response" of the forecast in periods 3 and 8 when you change alpha?

   b. In order to further investigate the link between the value of alpha and the responsiveness of the forecast, with the alpha at 0.1, use your mouse to drag the demand for period 9 to 70 units. What happens to the demand forecast for period 10? Experiment by doing this for each value of alpha. How would you quantify the relationship between alpha and the impact a change in alpha has on the responsiveness of the forecast?

   c. Repeat your experiment, but examine the impact that a reduction in the demand at period 7 has on the forecast for period 8. How does the forecast respond to the drop in demand at various levels of alpha?

2. Make sure that all demand values are at their starting defaults. If they are not, bring them to their defaults by clicking on the "Reset" button.

   a. With the alpha value at 0.1, what are the current values for MFE and MAD? What do these numbers mean?

    b. Experiment to find the alpha value that provides the best value for the MAD. Identify the alpha value that provides the best MFE. Are they the same? Explain.

    c. If you were in Connie's position, which measure would be most important to you? Why?

3. Three months after the demand data above were collected, Connie gathered another 12 weeks of demand. The new demand is shown below:

Period	1	2	3	4	5	6	7	8	9	10	11	12
Demand	52	56	67	73	66	63	56	54	46	55	58	63

4. Enter the new demand into the table in the Simple Exponential Smoothing Model.

    a. With an alpha of 0.1, examine how the forecast responds to demand changes as demand increases (periods 1–4) and as demand decreases (periods 4–9). Explain your observations.

    b. As the demand appears to change directions at periods 4 and 9, explain how the value of alpha affects the ability of the forecast to keep up with the demand. Examine the period of increasing demand and the period of decreasing demand. During these times, what happens to the bias of the forecast? How does the alpha affect the bias during these short periods?

    c. Based on your observations of simple exponential smoothing when demand is increasing and when demand is decreasing, explain why simple exponential smoothing is not recommended when the time series contains a trend.

The Trend Enhanced Exponential Smoothing Model

Trend adjusted exponential smoothing incorporates trend into the exponential smoothing forecast through the use of an additional smoothing constant. The model treats trend and random fluctuation components quite separately. In the calculation of the trend enhanced exponential smoothing forecast, the smoothed forecast is calculated exactly as in simple exponential smoothing. A trend component (T_t) is then added. T_t is computed by adding to the previous trend component (T_{t-1}), a weighted difference between the previous two trend adjusted forecasts and the previous trend. The second smoothing constant (β) determines the weight used.

Exhibit 1.3 shows the Trend Enhanced Exponential Smoothing Model.

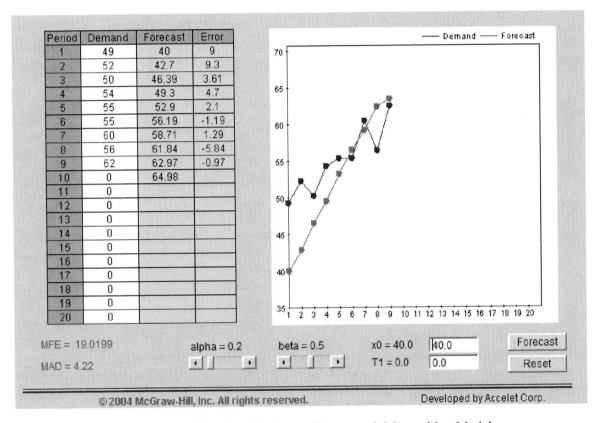

EXHIBIT 1.3 Screen View of the Trend Enhanced Exponential Smoothing Model

Interactive Case

Forecasting Demand for New Audio Products

Stan's Digital Audio sells audio accessories for MP3 players through several on-line auction services. He recently introduced a new product that transmits from any MP3 player to any FM radio within 10 feet. He orders his products at low cost directly from an Asian distributor, but must wait three weeks for delivery. This creates problems for new products with uncertain demand. Stan doesn't want to order too few or he will risk losing sales to competitors. However, if he orders too many, he can be stuck with products he can't move. The demand for the MP3 FM transmitter appears to have a sharply increasing trend, but also has a random component. Stan has collected demand data for the past nine weeks. He has decided to test trend enhanced exponential smoothing on his past demand to see if it is an effective forecasting tool.

Week	1	2	3	4	5	6	7	8	9
Demand	49	52	50	54	55	55	60	56	62

Analysis

1. Make sure the starting default values for the Trend Enhanced Exponential Smoothing Model match the demand above. The alpha should equal 0.1 and the beta should equal 0.5. If they do not, click on the "Reset" button.

    a. Do you agree with Stan's assessment of the trend and randomness in the data? Compare the red forecast data to the blue demand data with the alpha and beta values at their starting defaults. Describe the relationship between the two.

    b. With the alpha value at 0.2, manipulate the beta value, observing what happens to the forecast as beta is changed. At different beta values, drag a blue demand "dot" and observe what happens to the forecast. Describe the impact the beta value has on forecast response.

    c. With the beta set at various values, change the alpha value and observe what happens. Starting with low alpha values and progressing to high ones, drag a blue demand "dot" and observe how the forecast responds. Based on your observations and a close examination of the formula for calculating trend enhanced exponential smoothing, describe how the alpha and beta values interact to determine the forecast's responsiveness.

2. Set the demand and smoothing constants back to their starting defaults by clicking on the Reset button.

    a. By changing the alpha values and beta values separately, observe the forecast accuracy measures (MFE and MAD). Which seems to be most affected by changing the alpha? Which seems to be most affected by changing the beta?

    b. Which of the two measures should be most important for Stan to monitor? Which combination of alpha and beta values do you think provides the best forecast performance?

The Linear Trend Equation Model

The linear trend equation uses the time period as the independent variable in a simple linear regression model. It computes the formula of the best-fitting line through the data, and by extending that line into the future, provides forecasts of the future impact trend has on the data. That best-fitting line, often called the "trend line," is graphed with the demand data. The trend line takes the form $Y = a + bt$, where Y is the demand, a is the y intercept, b is the slope, and t is the time period. In addition to allowing the user to change demand values, the model also allows the user to drag demand, making it easy to see the impact of demand changes.

Exhibit 1.4 shows the Linear Trend Equation Model.

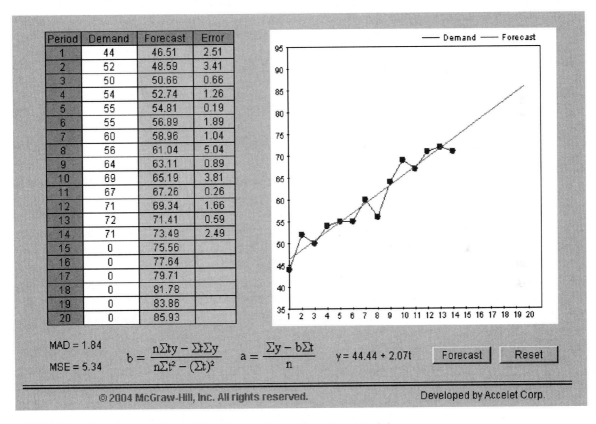

Period	Demand	Forecast	Error
1	44	46.51	2.51
2	52	48.59	3.41
3	50	50.66	0.66
4	54	52.74	1.26
5	55	54.81	0.19
6	55	56.89	1.89
7	60	58.96	1.04
8	56	61.04	5.04
9	64	63.11	0.89
10	69	65.19	3.81
11	67	67.26	0.26
12	71	69.34	1.66
13	72	71.41	0.59
14	71	73.49	2.49
15	0	75.56	
16	0	77.64	
17	0	79.71	
18	0	81.78	
19	0	83.86	
20	0	85.93	

$MAD = 1.84$

$MSE = 5.34$

$$b = \frac{n\Sigma ty - \Sigma t\Sigma y}{n\Sigma t^2 - (\Sigma t)^2} \qquad a = \frac{\Sigma y - b\Sigma t}{n} \qquad y = 44.44 + 2.07t$$

Forecast   Reset

Developed by Accelet Corp.

EXHIBIT 1.4   Screen View of the Linear Trend Equation Model

Interactive Case

Using Linear Trend Analysis to Project Demand Growth

North Mountain, a small Midwestern ski resort, offers a variety of passes to entice skiers to the slopes on weekdays. One pass allows skiers to ski on any weekday. A cheaper pass allows skiers to ski one day per week, on any weekday. An even cheaper annual pass allows skiers to select any day of the week, and then the skier can ski on that day every week. The cheapest pass of all allows skiers to ski every Tuesday. Sales of the "Tuesday only" pass have increased since its inception 14 years ago. Abigail Svenson, North's business manager, has decided to analyze the demand to help her determine if other passes should be created.

Analysis

Period	1	2	3	4	5	6	7	8	9	10	11	12	13	14
Demand	44	52	50	54	55	55	60	56	64	69	67	71	72	71

1. Make sure the demand values are at the startup defaults shown above. Record the formula for the trend line.

   a. An important early step in linear trend analysis is to remove outliers. Outliers are data points that are very unusual and should be eliminated from the time series because of their negative effect on the accuracy of the forecast. Outliers can have a significant impact on the forecast when using a linear trend equation, and that impact can depend on the location of the outlier. Do any of the data points in the 14 years of data appear to be outliers? Explain your answer.

   b. Drag the demand for period 2 from 52 to 62. What is the impact of that change on the formula for the trend line? What is the impact on forecast accuracy?

   c. Set the period 2 demand back to 52. Now drag the demand for period 5 from 55 to 65. What is the impact of that change on the trend formula? What is the impact on forecast accuracy?

   d. Set the period 5 demand back to 55. Now drag the demand for period 9 from 64 to 72. What is the impact of that change on the trend formula? What is the impact on forecast accuracy?

   e. Summarize the impact an outlier has on the formula for the trend and on the MFE and MAD. What clues would you look for in the MAD or MFE to indicate the presence of an outlier in the data?

2. Whenever the linear trend equation is used, the number of periods to include in the analysis is critical. Trends change over time. Using too much data results in the forecast's not responding to changes in trend. Using too little data runs the risk of the trend line's changing as a result of random fluctuations that really don't represent changes in the trend. Click on "Reset" to get the demand back to its starting default values.

   a. Click on "Forecast" and observe the graph. The trend equation is $44.44 + 2.07t$. Record the MAD and MFE. Clearly this is an upward trend, rising just over 2 units per period. What is the forecast for period 20?

   b. Abigail decided to use only the most recent 9 periods to compute the linear trend equation. To do this, change periods 10 through 14 to "0" and enter the following demand data for periods 1 through 9:

Period	1	2	3	4	5	6	7	8	9
Demand	55	60	56	64	69	67	71	72	71

3. Again, click on "Forecast" and observe the results. What is the new equation for the trend line? What are the new MAD and MFE? What is the forecast for period 20? Explain what happened.

The Simple Linear Regression Model

Demands for products and services are often related to an external variable. For example, soft drink sales at a ball game might be related to how hot the day is. New home construction might be related to interest rates. In these situations, forecasters can use the relationship between the demand and the extrinsic variable to create a causal model for forecasting demand. Simple linear regression identifies the linear relationships between the extrinsic or independent variable (on the x-axis) and the demand or dependent variable (on the y-axis) and calculates the formula for the best-fitting line through the data. The formula for the best-fitting line takes the form

$$Y = a + bx$$

where a = the Y intercept, b = the slope of the line, and x = the value of the independent variable.

Exhibit 1.5 shows the Simple Linear Regression Model.

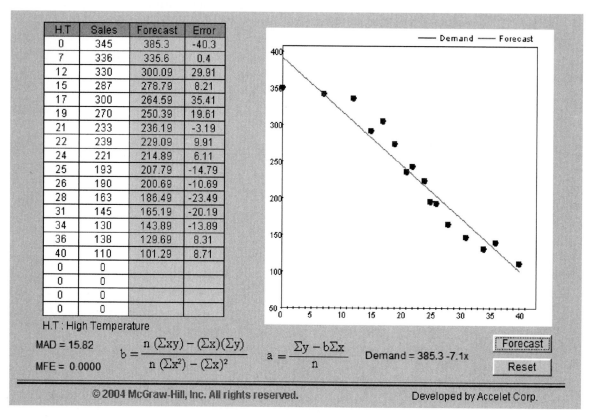

EXHIBIT 1.5   Screen View of the Simple Linear Regression Model

Interactive Case

Causal Forecasting with Simple Linear Regression

Abigail Svenson, North Mountain Ski Resort's business manager, monitors sales of all concessions in the ski lodge in an effort to keep adequate stocks of food and drink but also to prevent inventory levels from being excessive. Hot cocoa creates an interesting problem for kitchen staff. The hot cocoa machine is "loaded" with powder at 10 a.m. It is cleaned every night and powder remaining in the machine is discarded. Last winter, in an effort to develop a method for forecasting hot cocoa and reduce the amount of cocoa powder being thrown away, she monitored sales of hot cocoa and daily "high" temperature. Her data are presented below:

High temp	0	7	12	15	17	19	21	22	24	25	26	28	31	34	36	40
Sales	345	336	330	287	300	270	233	239	221	193	190	163	145	130	138	110

Analysis

1. When using simple linear regression as a causal technique, one must be aware of all of the cautions that apply to the linear trend model. Outliers have the same impact. Using too many or too few data points in the analysis can have the same impact as well. Make sure the starting defaults on the model match the demand data provided above. If they do not, click on "Reset."

   a. Drag demand points up and down on the graph. How does the formula and regression line change points as points near the ends of the line are moved? What is the impact of moving data points near the middle of the line?

   b. What happens to the MAD as points are dragged away from the line? What happens to the MFE? Why is the MFE always 0?

   c. Suppose you made the calculation for using this technique, used it to forecast demand, and very quickly discovered that your forecast was biased. What would you suspect as a cause for the bias?

2. Set the values to the defaults by clicking on "Reset." Outliers can be caused by aberrations in demand or by an input error. Key entry error is common and can have a huge impact on forecast accuracy. Record the regression equation and the MAD and MFE values for the default demand.

   a. Suppose the first data point had been mistakenly keyed in as 41 instead of 14. What impact would this have had on the forecast?

   b. Explain the effects errors related to the Y intercept and errors related to the slope have on the MAD and MFE. Experiment with the model to reach your conclusions.

Unit 2

Financial Decision Making

Models in This Unit:

The Breakeven Model

The Variance Analysis Model

Unit 2 contains two financially oriented interactive models. The **Breakeven Model** is a general-purpose decision-making tool used to aid in decisions characterized by alternatives with different fixed and variable costs. The model demonstrates how fixed and variable costs associated with different alternatives affect the result by allowing the user to change the inputs and view the impact graphically.

The **Variance Analysis Model** enhances the understanding of how price and usage variances interact to form the total variance, providing a focus for improvement of the total variance.

The Breakeven Model

Many decisions involve two types of costs. *Fixed costs* are unrelated to the volume of output and include such costs as facility construction or startup costs. *Variable costs* are related to volume of output and include such costs as material and transportation costs. The analysis of decision alternatives in these situations is known as *breakeven analysis*. When fixed costs are high relative to variable costs, large volumes are needed to spread the fixed costs over a large number of units. However, when variable costs are high, smaller volumes are more advantageous. Breakeven analysis identifies the volumes that support different combinations of fixed versus variable costs.

The Breakeven Model presents an interactive environment for a three-alternative decision scenario. The user can change fixed and variable costs of each alternative's cost curve by dragging the colored dots on the left and right of the line to see the impact on the output graph. The user can also drag the "n" line to investigate the three costs for any value of *n*. As the lines are dragged, all related volumes change.

Exhibit 2.1 shows the Breakeven Model.

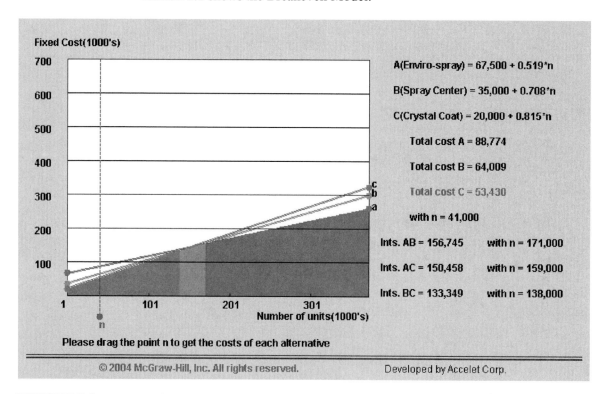

EXHIBIT 2.1   Screen View of the Breakeven Model

Interactive Case

Identifying the Most Economical Spray Facility for SportsExchange

SportsExchange is a regional refurbisher of sporting goods equipment. It specializes in upgrading football equipment that it receives from high schools and colleges. The equipment is brought in during the late winter and returned during the summer. Processes used by SportsExchange include sewing pants and jerseys, replacing pads, repairing and painting helmets, and replacing laces, snaps, and elastic in pants. The most expensive process for SportsExchange is painting helmets. Regulations that control worker safety and environmental emissions mandate a paint room that manages fumes effectively. In order to continue in its lucrative business, SportsExchange is required to invest in a new state-of-the-art painting facility. Maria Hinson, the SportsExchange owner, has identified three manufacturers of turnkey spray booths. The fixed and variable costs associated with each of the three alternatives are presented below:

Alternative	Fixed Cost	Variable Costs
A: Enviro-Spray	$67,500	$.519 per unit
B: Spray Center	$35,000	$.708 per unit
C: Crystal Coat	$20,000	$.815 per unit

Analysis

1. With the fixed and variable costs set to the values shown above, drag the "n" line to the volume of production desired.

   a. Maria Hinson has predicted that SportsExchange will need to refinish 156,000 helmets. What is the total cost, for each of the alternatives, of refinishing that quantity?

   b. If the fixed cost of Alternative C (Crystal Coat) is reduced to $15,000, what happens to the cost of producing 156,000 units on that alternative? What happens to the relative attractiveness of Alternative B (Spray Center) if Crystal Coat's fixed costs are reduced by $15,000?

   c. Assuming that the fixed costs for Enviro-Spray, Spray Center, and Crystal Coat are as originally stated ($67,500, $35000, and $20,000), what must the fixed cost of Enviro-Spray be reduced to in order for it to be the low-cost alternative with a demand of 156,000 units?

2. Reset the fixed and variable costs to their startup default values.

   a. Maria believes her forecast of 156,000 units demand for next year should be accurate to within 20 percent. What are the implications of a 20 percent error in either direction?

    b. If the company wishes to negotiate to lower the cost per unit for Spray Center, could it ever be the low-cost alternative for producing 260,000 units?

3. Set the values to the default settings by clicking your browser's "Refresh" button. Record the equations and the intersection points for all three alternatives.

    a. Crystal Coat has a new design that has lowered fixed costs to $15,000, but variable costs are increased to $0.903 per unit. How does this change the relationships among the three alternatives? How does this change the impact of Maria's demand forecast accuracy?

    b. Using the costs associated with Crystal Coat's new design, what must the variable costs for Enviro-Spray drop to for it to be the low-cost alternative at 156,000 units?

4. The fixed costs are often quite easy to determine, but variable costs can be difficult to predict. A small error in projecting the variable cost can make what seemed to be a correct alternative choice end up being the wrong one. We have seen the potential impact of inaccuracy in Maria's demand forecast, but it is also important to understand the impact of inaccuracy in predicting variable costs. Set the fixed and variable costs to their startup defaults.

    a. Spray Center is the low-cost alternative at Maria's expected production level, but the range of volumes where Spray Center is the low-cost alternative is actually quite narrow. At a fixed cost of $35,000 and variable costs just under 71 cents per unit, Spray Center appears to be a "no-brainer" for the best choice if demand is expected to be 156,000 units. However, a closer look at variable costs may give different results. What happens if the variable costs for Spray Center go up $0.02 to $0.728? Do you think being off by $0.02 on a variable cost of approximately $0.71 is very likely to happen?

    b. A shift in the variable costs of Spray Center can cause it to disappear as a low-cost alternative. Reset the variable costs of Spray Center back to $0.708. Being wrong on the variable cost predictions for other alternatives can also affect the fate of Spray Center. Once again, with the fixed and variable costs set at their startup defaults, take a close look at the range of low-cost demand for the Spray Center alternative. We have seen what can happen to this range when the Spray Center variable costs are inaccurate. Let's examine the impact of inaccuracies in predicting the variable costs for the other two alternatives. Suppose the variable costs for Enviro-Spray were inaccurate and, instead of $0.519 per unit, were actually $0.505 per unit, less than 2 cents lower. What happens to Spray Center as an alternative?

    c. Set the fixed and variable costs back to the startup defaults. How sensitive is Spray Center to inaccuracies in predicting variable costs for Crystal Coat? How low must Crystal Coat variable costs be to exclude Spray Center as an alternative?

The Variance Analysis Model

Variance analysis is used to compare what should happen to what actually did happen, particularly when monitoring and controlling productive processes. Such comparisons are made for materials consumed, output provided, and money spent on inputs and play a significant role in many operations decisions. In a typical situation, actual and standard quantities consumed and actual and standard prices for those items consumed provide the inputs for determining price variance, usage variance, and total variance. The Variance Analysis Model provides a visual mechanism for understanding the relationships among price variance, usage variance, and total variance. In this model, the user can modify actual price, standard price, actual usage, and standard usage by dragging the top edges of four bars. When these inputs are changed, the affected variances are highlighted and the new variance values are provided.

Exhibit 2.2 shows the Variance Analysis Model.

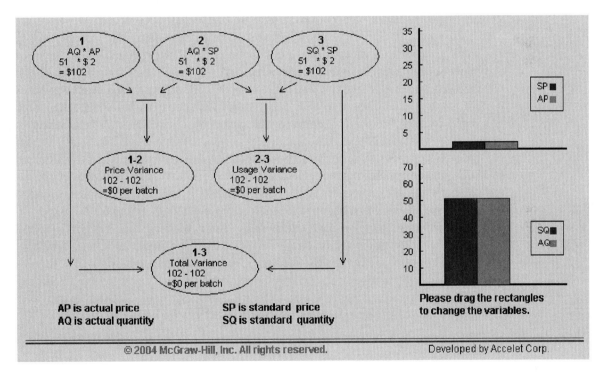

EXHIBIT 2.2   Screen View of the Variance Analysis Model

Interactive Case

Hollow Logs Furniture Tries to Control Costs

Hollow Logs, a premium quality furniture producer, started as a producer of custom home entertainment centers to fit unique room designs. After several years of customization, Alex Collins, the owner and head designer, developed a modular design that standardized much of the production, but still provided a significant amount of product flexibility. Despite its ability to customize, Hollow Logs' sales are dominated by one particular design, known as the Video Center. The Video Center shelf system, constructed out of red oak, comprises 58 percent of Hollow Logs' sales. As Alex has standardized components of his home entertainment centers, Hollow Logs has become more mechanized and labor costs per unit have dropped. Material costs, however, have remained high. High material costs are primarily a result of Hollow Logs' commitment to use real wood in their products. All of its home entertainment centers are solid wood, with the exception of the unit backs, which are oak veneered plywood, and the drawer bottoms, which are high density fiberboard.

Like most natural resources, wood quality varies from piece to piece and batch to batch. Hollow Logs uses only clear oak (no knots) in their products. The presence of knots in boards results in the boards being cut to shorter lengths, wasting wood. The more knots, the less "yield" Alex gets from the wood he purchases. Alex purchases red oak from a hardwood supplier and has paid $2 per board foot for more than three years. (A board foot is 12 inches by 12 inches by 1 inch thick.). Alex purchases $1'' \times 8'' \times 10$ feet boards (6.66 board feet per board) for $13.32. The Video Center Shelf System actually requires 43 board feet of red oak to construct, but waste from knots and defects results in the actual average consumption of 51 board feet of red oak per shelf. Alex considers $2 per board foot and 51 board feet per unit as his standard price and standard quantity for the Video Center shelf system.

Alex's wood supplier has traditionally purchased standing timber within a 100-mile radius of his mill in southern Indiana. As the larger trees have been harvested, however, the remaining trees are smaller and have more knots. These trees are expected to increase Alex's usage rates from 51 board feet to 64 board feet per unit for next year and the foreseeable future. Recognizing the impending increases in costs, Alex has begun to explore other alternatives for his wood supply.

Analysis

1. The startup default values are presented below:

   SP = $2   SQ = 51 board feet
   AP = $2   AQ = 51 board feet

   a. What is the current materials cost per unit?

   b. What will happen to the materials cost per unit if Alex's usage quantity increases from 51 to 64 board feet per unit?

   c. What is the usage variance that results from that change?

2. Alex's supplier has offered to transport red oak from northern Kentucky to increase the quality of the wood he ships. This wood is expected to reduce usage to 45 board feet per unit, but will cost $3 per board foot because of the increased transportation costs.

   a. What will the materials cost per unit if Alex uses this wood?

   b. What will be the price, usage, and total variances if the higher-quality wood is used?

   c. To what level will Alex need to reduce his actual quantity to make using the higher-quality oak more economical than using the poor-quality oak?

Unit 3

Capacity Management

Models in This Unit:

The Learning Curve Model

The Overbooking Model

The Aggregate Planning Model

Unit 3 provides three interactive models associated with capacity management. The first, the **Learning Curve Model,** addresses the phenomenon of learning curves, which reduce the time required to accomplish tasks as they are repeated. The model presents a typical project bidding scenario that requires incorporating learning into the projected costs of labor.

The second model is the **Overbooking Model,** which examines the decisions required when determining how many customers to overbook when making hotel reservations. The Overbooking Model allows the user to examine the total costs involved with various overbooking policies and to select the low-cost alternative.

The third model, the **Aggregate Planning Model,** examines a common approach to matching manufacturing capacity to demand. The Aggregate Planning Model allows the user to select among two aggregate planning strategies—demand chase and level production—and identify the low-cost alternative.

The Learning Curve Model

The Learning Curve Model provides an interactive laboratory for exploring the effects different learning rates can have on a typical bidding scenario. The model allows the user to specify the material cost per unit, labor hours per week, hourly salary rate, weekly overhead costs, time for the first unit, bid price, and the number of units in the order. The user sets the learning rate using the slider.

The system outputs include the learning rate selected, performance measures, project length, labor cost, overhead cost, materials cost, total cost, percent of total cost that is labor, percent of total cost that is overhead, percent of total cost that is materials, and profit. The learning rate affects the amount of labor required to complete the number of units specified in the order. The longer it takes to complete them, the higher the labor costs, and the lower the profit.

Exhibit 3.1 shows the Learning Curve Model.

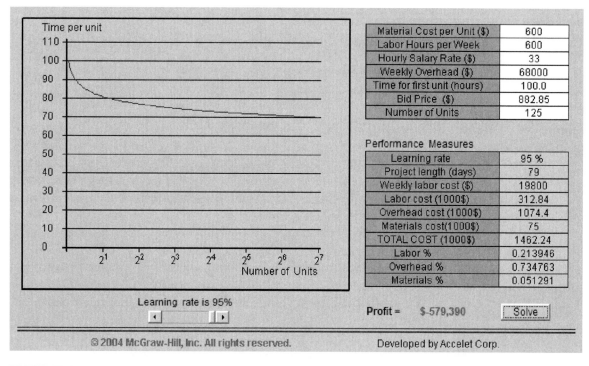

Material Cost per Unit ($)	600
Labor Hours per Week	600
Hourly Salary Rate ($)	33
Weekly Overhead ($)	68000
Time for first unit (hours)	100.0
Bid Price ($)	882.85
Number of Units	125

Performance Measures

Learning rate	95 %
Project length (days)	79
Weekly labor cost ($)	19800
Labor cost (1000$)	312.84
Overhead cost (1000$)	1074.4
Materials cost(1000$)	75
TOTAL COST (1000$)	1462.24
Labor %	0.213946
Overhead %	0.734763
Materials %	0.051291

Learning rate is 95%

Profit = $-579,390   [Solve]

EXHIBIT 3.1   Screen View of the Learning Curve Model

Interactive Case

Custom Precision Machining Wins (?) a Bid

Stan Eckles, owner of Custom Precision Machining (CPM), has struggled with the process of bidding for federal defense contracts. Sometimes he bids too high and doesn't get the bid. Other times, he bids too low and wins the bid but fails to make enough money to make it worthwhile. He can usually accurately estimate material costs, but he is very bad at estimating the cost of labor. His most recent attempt is a good example of this problem. He received the specs for a machined part used in a missile launch system, performed his typical analysis of the labor and material costs, and constructed his bid of $882.85 per unit for the 125 unit order. This bid was based on the following information, which sets the starting values in the Learning Curve Model:

Parameter	Default Value
Material Cost per Unit	$600
Labor Hours per Week	600
Hourly Salary Rate	$33
Weekly Overhead	$68,000
Time for First Unit (hours)	100

Analysis

1. Making sure the parameters are set at their proper starting values and the learning rate set at 95 percent:
   a. What is the project length at this learning rate? What is the expected profit?
   b. Improve the learning rate to 90 percent. What is the new project length? What is the new expected profit?
   c. What must the learning rate be in order for CPM to make a profit? What is the project length at that learning rate?
2. With the parameters still at the startup values, set the learning rate at 90 percent.
   a. The current time for the first unit is 100 hours. Enter a starting time for the first unit as 90. What is the new project length? What is the average time per unit produced (the total project length divided by the number of units in the order)?

   b. Reset the parameters to their startup defaults, with the learning rate at 90 percent. Increase the time for the first unit to 110 hours. What is the new project length? What is the average time per unit produced?

3. Set the parameters to their startup default values and set the learning rate to 90 percent.

   a. Record the project length, labor cost per day, total labor cost, labor cost as a percentage of the total cost, and profit.

   b. Improve the learning rate to 85 percent. Record the new values for project length, labor cost per day, total labor cost, labor cost as a percentage of the total cost, and profit.

4. Based on the outcomes, it appears that Stan has assumed a learning rate of 80 percent or better. Suppose his assumption is wrong and the best learning rate obtainable is 85 percent? Set the learning rate at 85 percent and all other parameters at their default values.

   a. If Stan wishes to make a profit of $220,000, what must the bid price be?

   b. At the bidding price needed to make $220,000 in profit, what will happen if his initial projection of an 85 percent learning rate was not correct? What are the risks of submitting the higher bid?

5. Set all values back to the startup defaults.

   a. What is the cost per unit at the 90 percent learning rate? What is the project length?

   b. Increase the number of units in the order from 125 to 200. What is the new project length? What is the new cost per unit? Increase the number of units from 200 to 300, and then incrementally by 100 units up to 1000 units. Compute the cost per unit at each quantity and graph the results. Describe the relationship between the number of units produced and cost per unit at a 90 percent learning rate.

   c. Perform the same experiment as in 5b, using an 80 percent learning rate. How do the results compare?

6. Set the parameters back to the default values. Set the learning rate at 90 percent.

   a. What is the labor cost as a percentage of the total cost?

   b. Increase the number of units in the order from 125 to 200. What is the percentage of labor cost as a percentage of the total? Increase the number of units from 200 to 300 and then incrementally by 100 units up to 1000 units. Record the labor cost as a percentage of the total cost at each quantity and graph the results. Describe the relationship between the labor cost percentage and the number of units produced at a 90 percent learning rate.

   c. Perform the same experiment as in 6b, using an 80 percent learning rate. How do the results compare?

The Overbooking Model

The Overbooking Model provides a dynamic platform for experimentation with a typical overbooking scenario. In a hotel room overbooking context, the model allows the user to manipulate the variables of overbooking policy (from 0 to 5), the vacant room cost, the bumping cost, and the probability of a given number of no-shows (0 to 5). Output for any trial overbooking policy shows the number of empty rooms and the number of customers bumped for any no-show condition, as well as expected costs and the total expected cost for the policy.

Exhibit 3.2 shows the Overbooking Model.

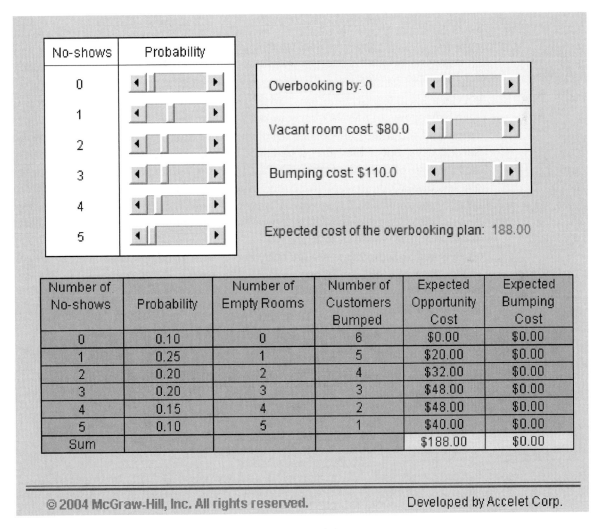

Number of No-shows	Probability	Number of Empty Rooms	Number of Customers Bumped	Expected Opportunity Cost	Expected Bumping Cost
0	0.10	0	6	$0.00	$0.00
1	0.25	1	5	$20.00	$0.00
2	0.20	2	4	$32.00	$0.00
3	0.20	3	3	$48.00	$0.00
4	0.15	4	2	$48.00	$0.00
5	0.10	5	1	$40.00	$0.00
Sum				$188.00	$0.00

Developed by Accelet Corp.

EXHIBIT 3.2   Screen View of the Overbooking Model

Interactive Case

Cutthroat Canyon Resort Battles No-Shows

Cutthroat Canyon Resort lies in a small canyon that runs perpendicular to the highway between Livingston and Gardner, Montana. The resort consists of a lodge with 18 rooms and 6 duplex cabins. Just down the road lies Yankee Jim Canyon, and beyond that, the North Entrance to Yellowstone National Park. Like all resorts in the vicinity of Yellowstone, Cutthroat Canyon serves two types of customers. The first, and most desirable from a business standpoint, is customers who make reservations to stay at the resort because they enjoy the amenities the resort has to offer—its peace and quiet, its excellent food, and its small-stream trout fishing. These customers often return year after year and stay for four or five days. The other customers certainly add to the revenue stream but are a more difficult lot to plan for. They are typically on their way to Yellowstone, pulling a monster RV, and find that, when they arrive at the north entrance, the campgrounds are full. They quickly learn that the spaces that are not reserved are taken on a first-come, first-served basis in the early morning. So they stay at Cutthroat Canyon for a night and then drive down to the park early to stake a claim on a campsite. If they get one, they move on; if they don't, they try again the next day. Many reserve a room for several days, but if they find a campsite in Yellowstone, they cancel at the last minute. This often leaves Bonnie DePuy, the resort owner, with empty rooms after she has denied others who have called in requesting a reservation. Bonnie's niece, who is working at the resort for the summer, has suggested using an overbooking approach she learned about in her operations management class at college. Bonnie is skeptical but is willing to listen.

Bonnie has approached a large neighboring resort and has negotiated an agreement to use it as lodging for any customers she "bumps" at a cost of $100. She has determined that the opportunity cost for an empty room in her lodge is $80. Historical records from the past two summers provide 200 days of no-show data. Those data are presented below and converted to probabilities.

Number of No-Shows	Frequency	Probability (%)
0	20	10%
1	50	25
2	40	20
3	40	20
4	30	15
5	20	10

Analysis

1. Make sure the defaults are set to match the parameters in the table on page 28. Evaluate each possible overbooking policy and record your results.

   a. What is the expected cost per night of not overbooking at all?

   b. What is the low-cost overbooking policy, given Bonnie's vacant room and bumping costs?

   c. Under the low-cost policy, what is the expected cost of bumping customers? What is the expected cost of vacant rooms? What is the expected total cost?

   d. Create a graph with "cost" on the y-axis and "number overbooked" on the x-axis. Graph the vacant room cost associated with each overbooking policy and the bumping cost associated with each overbooking policy. Describe the relationship between the two graphs.

   e. If Bonnie adopts the low-cost policy, what will be her daily expected savings over the current costs of not overbooking at all? What would she expect to save in the course of the 100-day season?

   f. What should she tell the neighboring resort in terms of the number of "bumped" customers to expect?

2. If Bonnie increases her room rental charges in the future, every dollar of increase would also increase the opportunity cost of a vacant room the same amount.

   a. Would it ever be justified to change to the policy to overbook by an additional person? How did you determine this?

3. Bonnie has learned that next summer the neighboring resort plans to decrease its costs to her by $20 per customer.

   a. If that happens, what should her overbooking policy be?

   b. What will the bumping costs have to be before it will result in a preferred policy of overbooking by one less person?

   c. Can the bumping costs be low enough to justify overbooking by one less person? Explain your answer.

4. Suppose Bonnie increases her room rental to $130 and the neighbor decreases the bumping cost by the amount identified in 3b.

   a. What would be the optimal overbooking policy?

   b. What would be the total expected costs per day?

   c. What would be the expected costs associated with no overbooking?

The Aggregate Planning Model

The Aggregate Planning Model solves an aggregate planning problem using two approaches: demand chase and level production. The primary input is the 12-month product demand in the first row of the table. In addition to modifying demand, the user can adjust sliding bars corresponding to inventory carrying costs and hiring/firing costs on a monthly basis, working days per month, working hours per day and hours to produce one unit to see the impact on the total cost for each of the two plans.

Exhibit 3.3 shows the Aggregate Planning Model.

Period	1	2	3	4	5	6	7	8	9	10	11	12	Totals
Demand	900	700	900	800	800	800	1300	1300	1100	1000	1000	800	11400
Demand Chase Strategy													
Hours req'd/day	315	245	315	280	280	280	455	455	385	350	350	280	31
Workers req'd/day	40	31	40	35	35	35	57	57	49	44	44	35	36
Hires req'd	0	0	9	0	0	0	22	0	0	0	0	0	
Fires req'd	0	9	0	5	0	0	0	0	8	5	0	9	
Hiring&Firing cost($)	0	3780	4950	2100	0	0	12100	0	3360	2100	0	3780	$32,170
Level Production Strategy													
Monthly output	950	950	950	950	950	950	950	950	950	950	950	950	
Beginning Inventory	0	50	300	350	500	650	800	450	100	-50	-100	-150	
Ending Inventory	50	300	350	500	650	800	450	100	-50	-100	-150	0	
Average Inventory	25	175	325	425	575	725	625	275	25	-75	-125	-75	
Carrying cost($)	275	1925	3575	4675	6325	7975	6875	3025	275	0	0	0	$34,925

Inventory carrying cost per month = $11   Firing cost = $420   Hiring cost = $550   [Solve]

◄ | ►   ◄ | ►   ◄ | ►

working days/month = 20   working hours/day/worker = 8   hours/unit = 7   [Reset]

◄| ►   ◄ | ►   ◄ | ►

EXHIBIT 3.3   Screen View of the Aggregate Planning Model

Interactive Case

Trading Off Workers for Inventory at DuraGlass

DuraGlass manufactures 14 different designs of fiberglass hulls for small sailboats. Demand for DuraGlass hulls comes from several different boat manufacturers and is seasonal with the fiscal year starting July 1. DuraGlass production capacity is dictated by the number of molds they own and the number of laborers trained in the production process. They currently own enough molds to meet peak capacity, but fluctuate their workforce to match high and low demand periods. Sylvia Collins, the new operations manager, wants to improve their planning process and complete an analysis of their options by comparing a demand chase and a level production strategy. She knows that training is time consuming and expensive, as are the out-placement services offered to employees who are laid off. She also knows that the large size of the hulls makes storing finished goods inventory expensive as well. Sylvia has gathered the costs and capacity information presented below:

Inventory Carrying Cost/Unit/Month	$11
Working Days/Month	20
Hours/Worker/Day	8
Firing Cost	$420
Hiring Cost	$550
Hours/Unit	7

Projected demand is:

Period	1	2	3	4	5	6	7	8	9	10	11	12
Demand	900	700	900	800	800	800	1300	1300	1100	1000	1000	800

Analysis

1. Make sure the startup values for the Aggregate Planning Model match the values above.
   a. Compare the costs of the demand chase and level production strategies. For each plan, describe where the costs come from.
   b. Given the current plans and their total costs, describe the relationship between inventory carrying costs and personnel (hiring and firing) costs.
   c. Despite the financial costs, what aspect of the level production strategy makes it an unattractive plan as it currently exists?
   d. The demand chase plan is a lower-cost plan according to the calculations. Are there any nonfinancial costs to consider? What impact would they have if they could be quantified?
2. Suppose Sylvia identifies warehouse facilities that reduce the inventory carrying costs to $8 per month.
   a. What happens to the relative attractiveness of the two plans?
   b. What happens to the relative attractiveness of the two plans if the production time per unit is reduced from 7 to 5 hours? Explain why this results in a cost reduction for one plan but not the other.

3. Set the variables back to the startup default values. Record the total cost for each plan.

   a. The demand provided is a forecast and we know that forecasts are often wrong. What effect on the two plans would occur if the demand for each month was actually 10 percent above the forecast demand. Why was the impact greater for one plan than for the other?

   b. Can you create a scenario in which a change in expected demand causes the financial attractiveness of the two plans to reverse?

Unit 4

Quality Management

Models in This Unit:

The X-bar and R-chart Model

Unit 4 consists of one model, the **X-bar and R-chart Model.** The X-bar and R-chart model is designed to explore the interaction between X-bar charts, R-charts, and process capability. As variability among the products in the sample changes, the relationship between the control limits and the specification limits change, as does the range of the sample. Process capability is defined by the relationship between the control limits and specification limits. For centered processes, C_p is used as the capability index. For noncentered processes, C_{pk} is used.

The X-bar and R-chart Model

The X-bar and R-chart Interactive Model provides an interactive environment for examination of statistical process control. The user can change two inputs. First, using the slider button, the user can change the level of process variability. This changes the standard deviation of the process (sigma). The user can also drag the center (grand mean) of the process up or down. The model provides capability index values for C_p and C_{pk}. As the user adjusts process variability, the value of sigma is changed, and the appropriate impact on the X-bar chart and R-chart takes place.

Exhibit 4.1 shows the X-bar and R-chart Model.

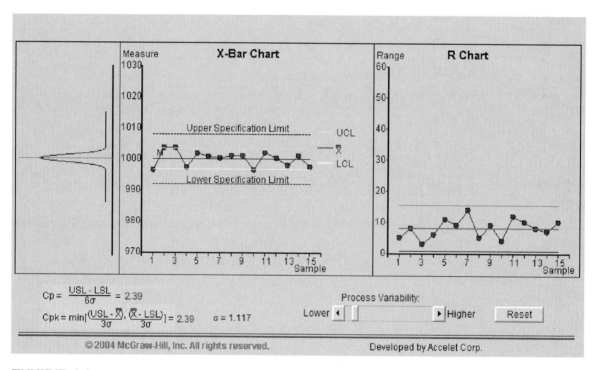

EXHIBIT 4.1 Screen View of the X-bar and R-chart Model

Interactive Case

Monitoring Variability at C&R Catalysts

C&R Catalysts produces chemicals that are used to speed up hardening or curing of paints, coatings, and fiberglass resins. They are a B2B supplier for paint companies as well as manufacturers who utilize fiberglass resins in the production of boats, automotive components, and sporting goods. One of C&R's competitive advantages is that it packages its chemicals to order to make their use easy and foolproof. One particular product, epoxy hardener 215, is used by several boat manufacturers in the production of sailboat hulls. Epoxy hardener 215 is combined with epoxy resin that is then applied to the fiberglass matting that has been formed around a hull mold. The matting soaks up the resin and hardens into the strong durable shell required for marine use. C&R works with each customer to determine the best resin batch size and the optimal amount of hardener needed to make its production process most effective. Precision is required because, if the batch size is too big, it takes too long to consume, and it hardens before being applied to the hull. This wastes material, and equipment (containers, spreaders, etc.) and is dangerous. In a container, the chemical reaction between the hardener and resin releases heat and can actually catch fire. If the batch size is too small, the glass layup process will not be able to finish before running out. If too much hardener is used, the resin hardens too quickly. If not enough hardener is used, the resin may never harden, remaining "sticky," and the hull would have to be scrapped.

Once C&R and the customer have determined the best amount of hardener to use, C&R packages the hardener in exactly that quantity. This eliminates the need for precise measuring, potential errors, and waste for the customer. For one customer, Raptor Boats, epoxy hardener 215 is packaged in precise 1000 milliliter quantities.

C&R has struggled with the precision required to consistently fill the disposable containers with the exact hardener quantities required. The process requires that the hardener be warm to reduce viscosity, and that the calibration of the filler machine be constantly monitored. Variation in volume can not only cause serious problems for customers, but can be very expensive for C&R. If a defective C&R product results in lost mold time or equipment damage, C&R reimburses its customer for actual costs incurred.

The filling process for hardener 215 1000-ml containers is currently centered at 1000 milliliters, with a standard deviation of 1.117 ml. This places the 3σ upper and lower control limits at 1003.351 and 996.649 respectively.

Analysis

1. The default values for the X-bar and R-chart Interactive Model should match the current conditions at C&R Catalysts, as shown below:

   Sigma = 1.117
   C_p = 2.39
   C_{pk} = 2.39

   The process should be exactly centered. If it is not, drag the red line on the normal curve to center it.

   a. At startup, notice that the values for C_p and C_{pk} are the same. Which capability index is of interest?

b. Raptor Boats has determined that, during the winter, if the hardener quantity stays within 8 ml of 1000 ml, its process works fine. As long as the contents are from 992 to 1008, everything is OK. Is C&R able to meet that expectation with its current process? Explain your answer.

2. During the summer, warmer weather causes the chemical reaction between the resin and hardener to speed up. This means that excess hardener would speed up the process too much. Raptor Boats has determined that as long as the hardener amount is between 996 and 1004 in the summer, their process will work.

   a. Is C&R able to meet that expectation with its current process? Explain your answer.

   b. During the winter, when the specifications are the most relaxed, what level of variability can C&R tolerate in its filling process? What is the sigma at that point?

   c. What happens to the R-chart when the variability is increased? What happens to the shape of the distribution to the left of the X-bar chart as the variability is increased?

3. C&R has detected that its process drifts because the warm hardener gradually changes the calibration on its filling equipment. As containers are filled, the quantity of hardener being put in each container gradually increases. This is a slow change but, if not monitored closely, could cause problems. Calibration is a difficult and time-consuming process, requiring the time of one of the engineers, so C&R would like to minimize it. Set the variability back to its default value of 1.117. The process should be centered. Current data indicate that after 200 containers the process has drifted, and the average output is no longer 1000, but is to the point that the upper control limit is right at the upper customer specification. This places the process mean (assuming sigma of 1.117, 3 sigma = 3.351, and $1008 - 3.351 = 1004.649$) at 1004.649.

   a. How could C&R benefit from using a noncentered process to minimize the time and cost associated with recalibrating equipment? Explain how this would work. Estimate how much they could reduce their recalibrations.

   b. Would C&R gain the same benefits in summer as they would in winter? Explain your answer.

   c. In order to gain similar benefits in summer, what would C&R need to do to their process?

Unit 5

Inventory Management and Scheduling

Models in This Unit:

Unit 5 consists of seven models. The first four models deal with inventory management. the **Economic Order Quantity Model** and the **Economic Order Quantity with Quantity Discounts Model** both deal with decisions of order quantity. The **Fixed Quantity Reorder Point Model** and the **Material Requirements Planning Model** represent inventory management systems and allow the user to explore interactions among parameters within those systems. The **Risk Pooling Model** and the **Bullwhip Effect Model** illustrate these classic supply chain concepts and allow the user to manipulate parameters and view results. The final model in this unit, the **Sequencing Rules Model,** presents an environment for comparing the performance of several sequencing rules.

The Economic Order Quantity Model

The Economic Order Quantity Model provides an interactive environment to explore how the input parameters of carrying cost, demand, and order cost affect the economic order quantity (EOQ). The EOQ calculation finds the minimum total cost for the combined holding and carrying costs. In the model, the user can change the values of the demand (D), the carrying cost (H), and the order cost (S) by manipulating three slider buttons. The outcome is presented graphically, with the order quantity on the x-axis and the total cost on the y-axis.

Exhibit 5.1 shows the Economic Order Quantity Model.

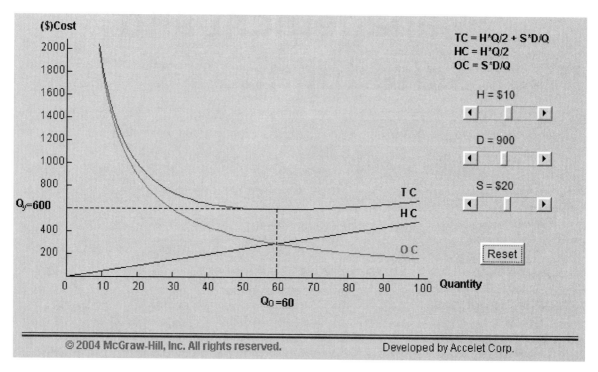

EXHIBIT 5.1   Screen View of the Economic Order Quantity Model

Interactive Case

MarketReach

MarketReach is a large contract calling center specializing in phone sales. It employs predominantly college students who like its flexible hours and relatively good pay. MarketReach not only makes phone contacts for its clients, but also coordinates any mailings that go out as follow-ups to successful calls. The type of employee utilized by MarketReach creates a high turnover rate. At any given time, MarketReach has approximately 300 employees, but loses about three per day.

MarketReach is continuously training new hires. Each new hire receives a set of training materials valued at approximately $35. History has shown that the demand for the training materials meets the assumptions of the economic order quantity, and management has decided that they should used that approach to determine order quantities.

Analysis

1. Demand for the training material packets is projected at 900 per year. Order cost is $20 and inventory carrying costs are $10 per packet per year. Make sure that the startup defaults on the Economic Order Quantity interactive model match these parameters.

   a. What is the economic order quantity at these parameter settings? Compute the total carrying cost and total order cost at these settings.

   b. From the shape of the total cost curve, do you think rounding the order quantity will have much of an impact on the total cost? Explain your answer.

2. MarketReach is negotiating with a different supplier of training materials. It appears that through that supplier the packets will be significantly cheaper, reducing the carrying costs. Set the parameters of the model to these values:

   a. What is the economic order quantity at these parameters?

Carrying Cost (H)	$6
Demand (D)	900
Order Cost (S)	$20

   b. Incrementally increase the carrying cost, $2 at a time, up to $16. Graph the impact on the economic order quantity. What is the relationship between the carrying cost and the economic order quantity?

3. If management can eliminate the paper invoicing associated with their ordering process, they believe they can reduce the order cost to $4. Set the parameters of the model to these values:

   a. What is the economic order quantity at these values?

Carrying Cost (H)	$10
Demand (D)	900
Order Cost (S)	$10

   b. Incrementally increase the order cost by $2 from $10 to $30. Graph the impact on the economic order quantity. Describe the relationship.

The Economic Order Quantity with Quantity Discounts Model

The Economic Order Quantity with Quantity Discounts Model enables the user to experiment with the parameters of the classic EOQ quantity discounts problem. The user sets the annual demand (D), the order cost (S), and the inventory carrying cost (H) using the three sliders. The pricing policies are set for the four discount levels using the four pricing policy sliders. The model calculates the total cost for the traditional EOQ quantity and for the smallest order quantities possible to receive each of the cheaper discounts.

Exhibit 5.2 shows the Economic Order Quantity with Quantity Discounts Model.

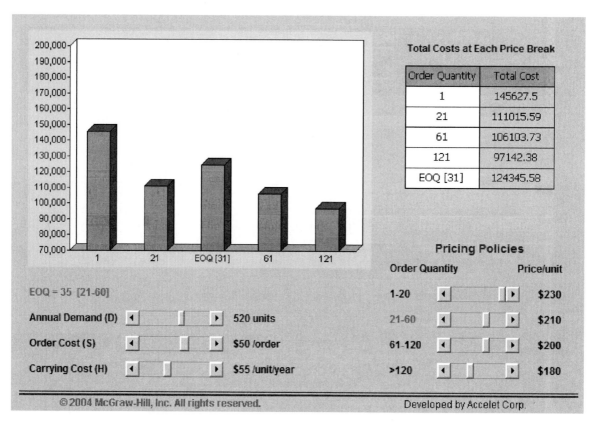

Total Costs at Each Price Break

Order Quantity	Total Cost
1	145627.5
21	111015.59
61	106103.73
121	97142.38
EOQ [31]	124345.58

EOQ = 35 [21-60]

Annual Demand (D) 520 units

Order Cost (S) $50 /order

Carrying Cost (H) $55 /unit/year

Pricing Policies

Order Quantity		Price/unit
1-20		$230
21-60		$210
61-120		$200
>120		$180

EXHIBIT 5.2   Screen View of the Economic Order Quantity with Quantity Discounts Model

Interactive Case

A Purchasing Decision for AutoAudio

AutoAudio sells and installs high-end automobile sound systems and is the largest installer in a large metropolitan area and the only one that can accommodate installations without appointments. The AutoAudio facility consists of eight drive-through installation bays, each equipped with complete sets of tools and an inventory of all brackets and installation hardware. AutoAudio buys its sound system components from several different suppliers, depending on the brand. One popular CD changer that is installed in the vehicle's trunk has a projected annual demand of 520 units. AutoAudio has just received word of better prices from a new supplier of that CD changer. The new supplier is offering the following prices:

Quantity	Price per Unit ($)
1–20 units	$230
21–60 units	210
61–120 units	200
>120 units	180

Auto Audio's carrying costs on this changer are $55 per unit per year. The order cost is $50 per order.

Analysis

Check to make sure the model parameters match the prices, demand, carrying cost, and order cost given above.

1. Examine the output values for the Economic Order Quantity with Quantity Discounts Interactive Model.

   a. What is the basic economic order quantity? In what price range is the EOQ?

   b. Based on the rules for determining the economic order quantity, what possible price ranges will likely contain the low-cost quantity?

   c. What quantity is the low-cost quantity? What is the total annual cost of ordering in that quantity?

   d. How much is saved by ordering at that quantity over the basic EOQ quantity?

2. Projected demands can often be wrong. This can result in an optimal order quantity changing or in a change in the projection of the total costs.

   a. If the forecast for demand for this CD changer is wrong (within the range of the model), does the optimal order quantity change?

     b. What happens to the total cost of ordering at the optimal quantity if demand is less than expected? How much does the total cost change?

     c. What happens to the cost of ordering at the optimal quantity if demand is greater than expected? How much does the total cost change?

3. The supplier of the CD changer is considering running a promotion to reduce inventory levels. The new prices will be:

Quantity	Price per Unit ($)
1–20 units	$200
21–60 units	190
61–120 units	180
>120 units	170

This will allow AutoAudio to reduce its price as well, resulting in an expected increase of demand by 80 units.

     a. What will be the optimal order quantity?

     b. What will be the total costs associated with this new pricing and new demand?

     c. AutoAudio normally sells this CD changer for $310. At the normal supplier pricing structure, and assuming a demand of 520 units, what would AutoAudio's annual profit be on this product?

     d. At the new pricing, assuming a demand of 600 units, AutoAudio is planning to reduce the selling price of the CD changer to $290. What will the profit be?

The Fixed Quantity Reorder Point Model

The Fixed Quantity Reorder Point Model illustrates the relationships present in a typical reorder point inventory system. In the model, the user can change the service level, the variability of demand, the replenishment lead time, and the order quantity by adjusting the sliding bars. Changes in any of the four parameters are reflected in changes in the system.

Exhibit 5.3 shows the Fixed Quantity Reorder Point Model.

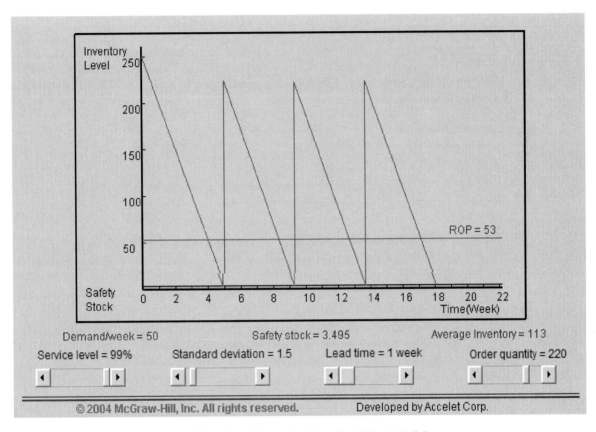

EXHIBIT 5.3   Screen View of the Fixed Quantity Reorder Point Model

Interactive Case

Managing Pillow Inventory at Wilson's Beds and Bedding

Wilson's Beds and Bedding is a large discounter of mattresses, beds, pillows, and linens. The pillow inventory is managed using a fixed quantity reorder point system. For the large down-filled pillow, the weekly demand averages a very stable 50 units, with a standard deviation of 1.5. The replenishment lead time for the large down-filled pillow is one week. Wilson's currently maintains a 99 percent service level for all of their pillows and orders the down-filled pillows in orders of 220 units.

1. Check the default values on the Fixed Quantity Reorder Point Model to make sure they match the values presented above.

   a. What is the reorder point for Wilson's large down-filled pillow?

   b. What happens to the reorder point if the replenishment lead time extends to two weeks?

   c. What happens to the reorder point if the standard deviation of demand shifts from 1.5 to 8?

   d. Reduce the service level from 99 percent to 95 percent. What impact does this have on the reorder point?

2. Safety stock is a function of the variability of demand (s) and the service level desired. The safety stock affects the average level of inventory because the average level of inventory is equal to one-half the order quantity plus the safety stock. Set the parameters of the model to the following values:

Service level	85 percent
Standard deviation	4
Replenishment lead time	2 weeks

   a. What is the reorder point and average inventory level at these parameters?

   b. Increase the service level to 89 percent. What happens to the reorder point and average inventory level? Increase the service level in 1 percent increments and graph the change in reorder point and average inventory level. Describe what is causing the change in the reorder point.

3. The safety stock contributes to the reorder point and the average level of inventory. If no variability existed from period to period, there would be no uncertainty of demand and no need for a safety stock. Set the parameters to the following values:

Service level	95 percent
Standard deviation	1
Replenishment lead time	3 weeks

   a. Record the values for the reorder point and average level of inventory. Incrementally change the standard deviation of demand by one-unit intervals, and record the corresponding changes in the reorder point and average level of inventory. Describe the relationship between variability of demand, reorder point, and average inventory level.

b. Set the parameters to the following values:

Service level	95 percent
Standard deviation	1
Replenishment lead time	1 week

c. Record the values for the reorder point and average level of inventory. Repeat the process of incrementally changing the standard deviation of demand by one-unit intervals, and recording the corresponding changes in the reorder point and average level of inventory. What impact does the replenishment lead time have on the relationship between variability of demand, reorder point, and average inventory level?

4. The reorder point is expected to satisfy demand during the replenishment lead time. The longer that lead time, the greater the demand, and the higher the reorder point will be. Set the parameters to the following values:

Service level	95 percent
Standard deviation	1
Replenishment lead time	1 week

a. What happens to the reorder point when the replenishment lead time is increased to 2 weeks? Three weeks? Four weeks? Why is the standard deviation of demand during the lead time changing?

b. What happens to the average level of inventory as you move from 1 week, to 2 weeks, to 3 weeks, to 4 weeks?

The Material Requirements Planning Model

The Material Requirements Planning Model provides an interactive environment for understanding how material requirements planning (MRP) logic works. The user can make changes to the master production schedule, the product structure, lead time, on-hand inventory level, and the lot-sizing policy used. Changes in any of those parameters are reflected in the timing and quantities for the planned order releases.

Exhibit 5.4 shows the Material Requirements Planning Model.

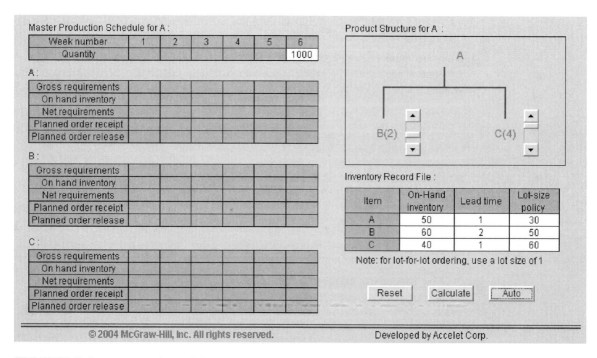

EXHIBIT 5.4   Screen View of the Material Requirements Planning Model

Interactive Case

Material Requirements for Rustic Furniture

Rustic Furniture is a producer of outdoor tables and chairs that are comprised of interlocking wooden components, requiring no fasteners, and allowing for quick setup and breakdown. The table (End Product A), for example, consists of two top sections (part "B"), and four legs (part "C"). The management of Rustic Furniture has not used material requirements planning in the past and is experimenting with a prototype to gain an understanding of how it works. Make sure the startup defaults in the Material Requirements Planning Model are consistent with those below:

1. The Master Production Schedule should show 1000 units in week 6.

Item	On-Hand Inventory	Lead Time	Lot-size Policy
A	50	1	30
B	60	2	50
C	40	1	60

   a. Given these parameters, what are the quantities and timing of the planned order releases necessary to produce the master production schedule?

   b. Why do the order release quantities not equal the net requirements?

   c. Reset the model, leaving all parameters the same, except change the lot-size policies to lot-for-lot by setting each equal to 1. What are the implications for carrying inventory when this is changed? What will be the implications for equipment changeovers in the future?

   d. Describe the relationship between the gross requirements for B and C and the planned order releases for A. Why are the gross requirements for B and C not dependent on the gross requirements for A?

2. Change the lead time for the end product from 1 week to 3 weeks.

   a. What are the implications for the timing of the planned order releases for B and C?

   b. Change the on-hand inventory for A to 1000. Why are there no gross requirements for B or C?

The Risk Pooling Model

The Risk Pooling Model demonstrates how the level of inventory in the supply chain is affected by where inventory is stored and the service level required of that inventory. Risk pooling is accomplished when the demand variability among a large number of supply chain entities is combined by storing inventory centrally, rather than at individual sites. The Risk Pooling Model demonstrates the effects of risk pooling on inventory level through the use of a distribution network with one central distribution center, two regional distribution centers, and four retailers. By selecting the service level and the storage location from the items on the pull-down lists, the user can see the effects on inventory levels at different locations and in total. The user can also edit the weekly demand and standard deviation for either product for each retailer, and then press the "Solve" button to see the impact.

Exhibit 5.5 shows the Risk Pooling Model.

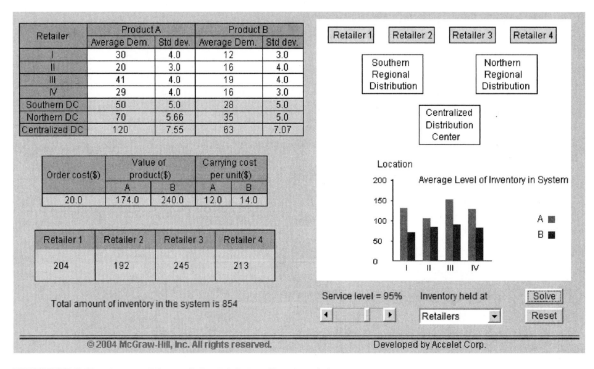

EXHIBIT 5.5   Screen View of the Risk Pooling Model

Interactive Case

Determining an Inventory Storage Strategy at Owen's Gourmet

Owen's Gourmet Shops has opened four retail stores in the suburban St. Louis area. Two are on the south side and two are on the north side. The southern stores are 20 miles from each other and 60 miles from the northern stores. The northern stores are also about 20 miles apart. Alvin Owen, the owner, expects to open at least eight more stores in the St. Louis area in the next five years. Frank Owen, son of the owner and inventory manager, is trying to decide between three inventory storage strategies. The first is to store all inventory at the retail stores. The second is to open two small distribution centers—one for the southern region and one for the northern region. Other than inventory on the shelves, all other inventory for each region would be stored in the two regional DCs. The third alternative is to lease one warehouse to be used as a central distribution center. Frank has selected two products, identified here as product A and product B, to serve as the basis for his study. The inventory carrying cost for product A is $12 per unit per year. The inventory carrying cost for product B is $14 per unit per year. Weekly average demand for each of these products at each store is presented below.

Retailer	Product A		Product B	
	Average Demand	Standard Deviation	Average Demand	Standard Deviation
I	30	4.0	12	3.0
II	20	3.0	16	4.0
III	41	4.0	19	4.0
IV	29	4.0	16	3.0

Analysis

1. Set the service level to 85 percent. Leave product demand and standard deviation values at the default levels.

   a. Compare the system inventory levels for the three alternative storage strategies of retailer, regional DC, and centralized DC. How do the inventory levels compare?

2. Increase the service level to 90 percent and perform the same comparison. Leave product demand and standard deviation values at the default levels.

   a. Compare the system inventory levels for the three alternative storage strategies of retailer, regional DC, and centralized DC. How do the inventory levels compare?

3. Increase the service level to 95 percent and perform the same comparison. Leave product demand and standard deviation values at the default levels.

   a. As the service level is increased, graph the change in inventory levels for the three storage location strategies.

   b. Explain the impact that the increase in service level has on the difference in inventory levels for the three alternatives.

4. Set the service level to 85 percent. Leave product demand at the default values. Increase each standard deviation by two units.

   a. What is the level of system inventory for each alternative inventory location? How has it changed as a result of the increase in demand variability?

   b. Incrementally increase the standard deviation two units at a time. Graph the results for each inventory storage location strategy.

   c. Explain the relationship between demand variability and the inventory level.

5. Change the service level to 90 percent and then 95 percent, monitoring the changes in inventory for each storage location alternative.

   a. What are the relationships among nearness of inventory to the customer, demand variability, and service level? What costs should be considered when making the decision about where to store inventory?

6. Frank has determined that, based on the value of the products, the average inventory carrying cost is $13 per year.

   a. What are the inventory carrying costs associated with each location strategy at a 95 percent service level? Given the locations of the stores and the distribution center alternatives, what other costs should be considered when the decision is made?

The Bullwhip Effect Model

The Bullwhip Effect Model demonstrates how the variability of demand is accentuated as one moves upstream in the supply chain. A simple three-tier supply chain (retailer, distributor, manufacturer) is used. Orders are generated by the retailer's order-up-to-level inventory system, which forecasts demand using a simple five-period moving average. Those orders become the demand for the distributor, who uses a similar inventory management system, which creates orders that become the demand for the manufacturer. The manufacturer's inventory management system creates orders for the supplier. The user can specify the mean and standard deviation for the retailer's demand as well as the replenishment lead time for the retailer's orders to the distribution center and for the distribution center's orders to the manufacturer. The model provides the actual standard deviation of demand and a graph of demand for each level in the supply chain.

Exhibit 5.6 shows the Bullwhip Effect Interactive Model.

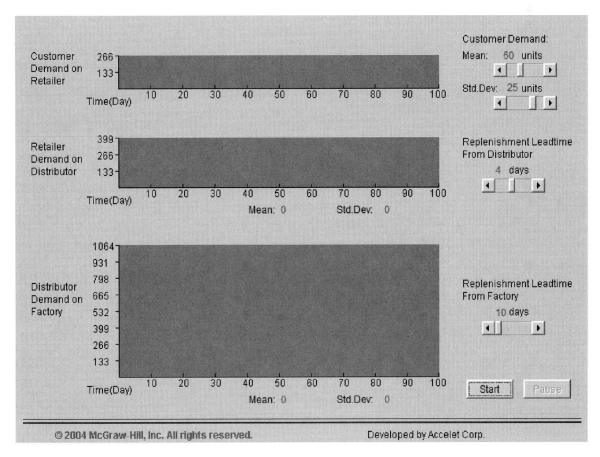

EXHIBIT 5.6   Screen View of the Bullwhip Effect Interactive Model

Interactive Case

Demand Variability in U-Save's Supply Chain

U-Save is a regional grocery store chain serving the Midwestern states. Most of the goods it sells are brand-name products. One supplier is examining the implications of supply chain management, particularly linking directly to its retailer's POS data, rather than having its inventory system driven by forecasts. Its consultants have told its managers that long lead times and forecasts are causing its demand to be far more variable than necessary. In order to gather information, U-Save has been asked to supply its daily demand for one representative product. The distribution center is providing its demand, as is the factory, to give the consultants an idea of what is happening in the entire system.

Analysis

1. Check the defaults to make sure the system is starting with the following parameters:

   Customer demand at retailer: Mean = 60, Standard deviation = 25
   Replenishment lead time from distributor to retailer = 4
   Replenishment lead time from factory to distributor = 10

   Start the simulation so that it can run 100 days of consumer demand.

   a. At the end of the 100-day run, what is the mean demand and standard deviation for the distributor?
   b. At the end of the 100-day run, what is the mean demand and standard deviation for the factory.
   c. Any time the graph shows a steep upward sloping line, it indicates that an order was received. During the 100 days, how many orders were received by the distribution center from the factory? How many were received by the factory from its supplier?

2. Change the replenishment lead time for orders from the distribution center to the retailer from 4 to 10 days. Run the simulation for 100 days.

   a. What happens to the mean and variability of demand at the distribution center and factory?
   b. What happens to the number of orders? Does it appear that there were any stockouts at the distribution center or at the factory?

3. Set standard deviation of demand at the retailer to 10, the replenishment lead time for the distributor to the retailer to 1, and the replenishment lead time from the factory to the distributor to 10.

   a. What happens to the mean and variability of demand at the distribution center and factory?
   b. What happens to the number of orders? Does it appear that there were any stockouts at the distribution center or at the factory?

4. Describe the relationship between the variability of demand upstream at the distribution center and factory and the variability of demand at the retailer.

5. Describe the relationship between the variability of demand and the replenishment lead time at each level of the supply chain.

6. Describe the relationship between order frequency, order size, and variability of demand.

The Sequencing Rules Model

The Sequencing Rule Interactive Model provides a quick and easy way to compare the performance of several traditional sequencing rules. The techniques included for comparison are earliest due date (EDD), shortest processing time (SPT), critical ratio (CR), and first-come, first-served (FCFS). The user has the option of using the default data or entering new data for estimated completion time and due date. The user must also select the number of orders to be sequenced. By selecting the rule to be applied and clicking on the "Schedule" button, the model resequences the orders and provides a color-coded Gantt chart of the resulting schedule. When orders are projected to be completed after their due date, a line showing the due date is also provided. Performance measures of total days late, number of orders late, and average lateness are provided.

Exhibit 5.7 shows the Sequencing Rules Model.

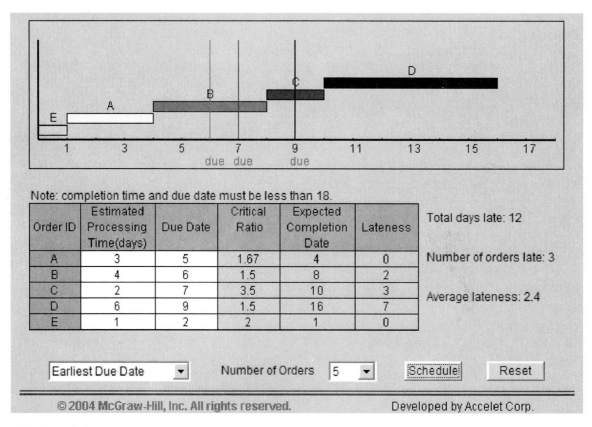

Note: completion time and due date must be less than 18.

Order ID	Estimated Processing Time(days)	Due Date	Critical Ratio	Expected Completion Date	Lateness	
A	3	5	1.67	4	0	Total days late: 12
B	4	6	1.5	8	2	Number of orders late: 3
C	2	7	3.5	10	3	
D	6	9	1.5	16	7	Average lateness: 2.4
E	1	2	2	1	0	

Earliest Due Date ▼   Number of Orders 5 ▼   Schedule   Reset

EXHIBIT 5.7   Screen View of the Sequencing Rules Model

Interactive Case

Sequencing Jobs at Jensen's Custom Auto Restoration

Jensen's Custom Auto Restoration specializes in refurbishing sports cars from the 1950s, 1960s, and 1970s. Jensen's capabilities range from mechanical engine work to body and paint projects. As a part of the cost estimation process, Bill Jensen estimates the number of days to complete each job and negotiates a due date based on the projected time to complete the project and the availability of necessary parts. History shows that Bill has been quite accurate at estimating time to complete various jobs. Bill wishes to evaluate the potential of using sequencing rules that differ from his typical "first-come, first-served" approach to sequencing restoration jobs.

Analysis

1. Use the default data for the five jobs to be sequenced, as shown below, and sequence the jobs by earliest due date.

Job ID	Estimated Completion Time	Due Date
A	3	5
B	4	6
C	2	7
D	6	9
E	1	2

   a. Record the performance measures and re-sequence by shortest processing time. How does the performance of the two rules compare on total days late, number of jobs late, and average lateness? Were you surprised by the results?

   b. Which rule would you select? Explain your answer.

2. Again, use the default data for the five jobs to be sequenced, and sequence the orders by the critical ratio rule. Record the performance measures.

   a. Resequence the orders by first-come, first-served and compare the results.

   b. Rank the four rules for each performance measure. How does the performance of the four rules compare?

3. As new jobs come in, they must be added into the sequence. Suppose that as Job B was completed, a new order arrived. Delete the estimated completion time and due date for job B and replace them with an estimated processing time of 8 and a due date of 17. Resequence the orders, again using shortest processing time. What position does that order take in the sequence? What happens to the performance measures?

4. Enter another order, in place of the current B order, that has a processing time that is longer than any of the current orders.

   a. What happens to it? What happens to the performance measures? What does this indicate for the shortest processing time rule? What is its flaw? How might you intervene to eliminate this problem?

5. A rule based on due date also makes sense, since the due date is one-half of the cause of an order being late. The most commonly used rule of this type is earliest due date (EDD). It basically gives priority to the order due the earliest.

   a. Earliest due date often provides the best results in terms of average lateness. Using the default values for five jobs, record the performance measures for the EDD sequence and compare the results to those of the first-come, first-served sequence.

   b. Add the sixth default order and reschedule. How does the performance change? Explain what happens to the sequence.

6. Compare the results of first-come, first-served, earliest due date, and shortest processing time for the default settings using 4, 5, and 6 orders. How to they compare?

7. The critical ratio rule combines information from the due date and the processing time of each order to compute a ratio of the due date to the expected processing time. The resulting ratio provides a picture of the amount of extra time available to process the order. An order that is already late will have a critical ratio less than 1. The larger the ratio, the more extra time available. The orders are scheduled by the ratio; smallest is first.

   a. Sequence the default values for five jobs using the critical ratio rules. Compare the results of the critical ratio rule to those of the EDD, SPT, and FCFS rules. How does it compare?

Facility Decision Models

Models in This Unit:

The Process-Oriented Layout Model

The Center of Gravity Model

Unit 6 consists of two models that relate to common facility-oriented decisions. The first, the **Process-Oriented Layout Model,** provides an experimental environment for examining the cost implications for alternative layouts of functional departments in a printing business. The second model, the **Center of Gravity Model,** examines the relationships and logic involved in locating a central distribution center to minimize transportation costs to retailers.

The Process-Oriented Layout Model

Process-oriented layouts are used when the producer needs flexibility to accommodate variable routings of products or customers through the system. While the flexibility is an advantage over product-oriented layouts, material transportation or customer movement from one department to another can be detrimental to productivity and service quality. In most process-oriented layouts, despite variability of routings, some pairs of departments are naturally more important to locate next to each other. Not surprisingly, if the design of the facility can take advantage of known relationships between departments, transportation and associated costs can be reduced. The Process-Oriented Layout Model allows the user to test various alternative layouts in a six-department facility and get immediate feedback on transportation costs.

Exhibit 6.1 shows the Process-Oriented Layout Model.

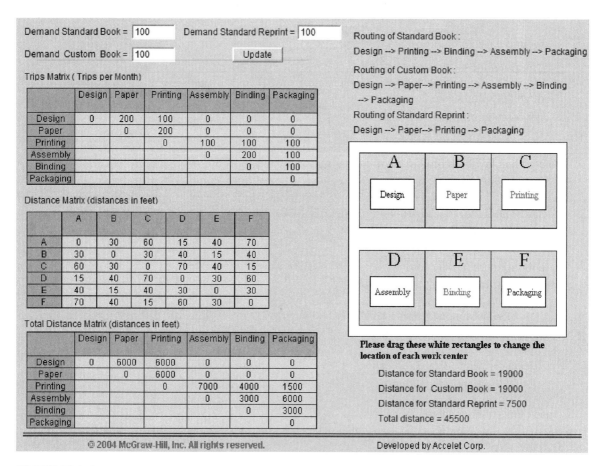

EXHIBIT 6.1   Screen View of the Process-Oriented Layout Model

Interactive Case

Redesigning Redi-Print

Redi-Print is a small printing and binding business specializing in small-volume runs of books. Its primary expertise is in printing and design, but it is also gradually moving into the assembly and binding of books. Many of its customers are colleges and universities, but it also produces books for other nonprofit organizations. Its book production consists of three standard outputs. The standard book is the typical job that begins in the design room. The book design is then sent to the paper department where paper type is determined and the proper paper is ordered. When the paper has been received, the design and the paper are sent to binding, where the appropriate cover type and spine thickness are determined. The order then moves to the printing department, where the pages are actually printed. Pages are shrink-wrapped for protection in the packaging department and then are sent to a subcontractor, who produces the cover and assembles the completed book.

The second possible product configuration is the custom book. The custom book also starts in the design department. The design is sent to the paper department for paper assignment and then to printing. Following printing, the printed pages are sent to assembly for insertion into a hard cover. Books then go to binding, where pages are permanently attached to the cover spine. From there the books go to packaging where they are shrink-wrapped and boxed.

The third product configuration is the standard reprint. The standard reprint needs no design work. The order fulfillment process starts in the paper department, which has already received preprinted pages from the books publisher. The pages then go to the binding department for insertion into the cover. Books then go to binding, where pages are permanently attached to the cover spine. From there the books go to packaging where they are shrink-wrapped and boxed.

As their work changes and they become more of a full-service printer, Redi-Print managers are considering a reorganization of their facility to better meet order routings and reduce costs. The current product mix is equally distributed among the three products.

User input parameters in this model are restricted to the demand for each of three products and the locations of each of six departments. The routings for each of the three products are provided. The number of trips required between departments is a function of the monthly demand for a product and the product's routing. So if a particular product routing specifies transporting the order from paper storage to printing, and there was a demand of 200 orders per month, there would be 200 trips from paper to printing per month resulting from that product. The other products may add more, depending on their routings. Total distances are computed as the number of trips between two departments per month multiplied by the distance between the two departments, as determined by a particular layout alternative. Departments can be moved from one location "room" to another by simply dragging the department to another location. When a department is dragged to another room, the department already there moves to the room just vacated. By swapping departments in this manner, any layout desired can be created.

Analysis

1. Make sure the demand settings and layout are at the starting defaults of:

    Standard Book Orders = 100
    Customer Book Orders = 100
    Standard Reprint Orders = 100.

    The default layout is:

Location	Department
A	Design
B	Paper storage
C	Printing
D	Assembly
E	Binding
F	Packaging

    a. Given the routings presented, identify a department that you think should be as close as possible to the paper storage department. Does "as close as possible" mean adjacent to each other or across the hall from each other? Why do you think the two departments should be as close as possible to each other? Make a change to the layout so that they are actually as close together as they can be. What happens to the total distance for the layout when this move is made?

    b. Identify another department that should be close to the paper department. What is your rationale for it being close to printing? Move it as close as possible, while maintaining the relationship between paper and the department you identified for 1a. Is the total distance improved? If so, by how much?

    c. What happens if the two departments you identified to be close to printing swap places? Is the total distance reduced or increased? Explain why it is more important for one than the other to be closest to paper.

2. Start with your layout as it was at the end of 1 above.

    a. Record the layout. What is its total monthly distance?

    b. Examine the routings. Can you identify any other changes that might improve the layout? Try them. What is the best layout you can come up with? What is the total distance? Explain, in terms of the demand and the routings, why your changes resulted in an improvement.

3. Set the layout back to the starting defaults.

   a. What is the total distance associated with the standard book product? Identify the layout that minimizes the total distance for the standard book. What is it?

   b. Identify and record the layout that minimizes the total distance for the custom book.

   c. Identify and record the layout that minimizes the total distance for the standard reprint.

4. Set the demand defaults back to 100 for each product and set the layout back to its starting default. The routings for the three products are:

   Standard Book: Design→Printing→Binding→Assembly→Packaging
   Custom Book: Design→Paper→Printing→Assembly→Binding→Packaging
   Standard Reprint: Design→Paper→Printing→Packaging

   a. Examine the three routings closely. Use a matrix similar to the one below and rate the importance of being close together for each pair of departments. Use ratings such as "absolutely necessary," "very important," "important," and so forth.

	Paper Storage	Design	Binding	Printing	Assembly	Packaging
Paper Storage	xxxxxx					
Design	xxxxxx	xxxxxx				
Binding	xxxxxx	xxxxxx	xxxxxx			
Printing	xxxxxx	xxxxxx	xxxxxx	xxxxxx		
Assembly	xxxxxx	xxxxxx	xxxxxx	xxxxxx	xxxxxx	
Packaging	xxxxxx	xxxxxx	xxxxxx	xxxxxx	xxxxxx	xxxxxx

   b. Create guidelines for arranging the layout by matching each of your ratings with one of the following potential department relationships:

   Immediately across from each other.
   Immediately next to each others.
   Diagonal across and one over from each other.
   Opposite ends of the same side.
   Diagonal opposite ends of the hall.

   c. Arrange a layout that satisfies your guidelines.

   d. Can more than one layout be created to meet your guidelines? If so, what are they? When you actually arrange them, do they all have the same total distance?

5. The composition of demand and the proportions of the various products can have a significant impact on transportation of goods from one department or work center to another. In a dynamic environment with frequent changes in the product mix, the layout

cannot be changing all of the time to keep up. However, when identifying the best layout, it is important to consider the layout that will best meet the most likely mix of products. Arrange the layout as below:

Location	Department
A	Design
B	Binding
C	Assembly
D	Paper
E	Printing
F	Packaging

a. This layout is very good when the product mix is 100 for each product. Change the product demands to Standard Book = 100, Custom Book = 250, and Standard Reprint = 100. What is the total distance for this product mix with this layout?

b. How can the layout be improved? Identify the best layout for this product mix. What is the total distance for the best layout? Explain why your improvements worked.

c. Identify the worst possible layout for this product mix. What is the total distance? How does it compare to the best layout for this product mix?

The Center of Gravity Model

Location decisions for central warehouses that ship products to a number of retailers often have a goal of minimizing transportation costs. Total transportation costs associated with a time period are a function of the distance traveled to make a shipment and the number of shipments made during the period. The center of gravity method minimizes the total costs associated with shipments by finding the central location for the distribution center, given the number of shipments.

The Center of Gravity Model allows the user to manipulate the environment in which the center of gravity technique would be used. In this environment, a central distribution center is being located among six retailers with varying shipments. By changing the number of shipments, or by dragging a retailer to a new location, the user can see the effects on the center of gravity location decision.

Exhibit 6.2 shows the Center of Gravity Model.

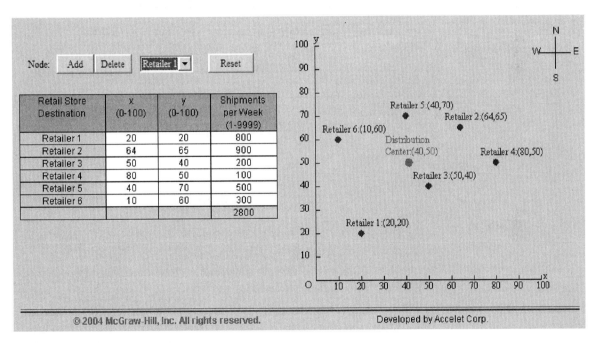

Developed by Accelet Corp.

EXHIBIT 6.2   Screen View of the Center of Gravity Model

Interactive Case

A New Customer for RLX Logistics

RLX Logistics is a third-party logistics (3PL) provider for several retail chains. RLX builds or, when possible, leases warehouse facilities to provide a regionally centralized delivery point for products, stores them, and ships them as needed to individual retail stores. RLX has recently signed a contract to provide 3PL services to a locally owned six-store sporting goods chain in the Chicago area. An empty and available warehouse was been identified in nearly the exact location specified by the center of gravity analysis.

By placing all retail destinations on a grid, the center of gravity analysis is able to identify the point on that grid that offers the lowest total transportation costs, given distances and the quantity of shipments necessary.

The default values are:

Retail Store Destination	X (0–100)	Y (0–100)	Shipments per Week (1–999)
Retailer 1	20	20	800
Retailer 2	64	65	900
Retailer 3	50	40	200
Retailer 4	80	50	100
Retailer 5	40	70	500
Retailer 6	10	60	300

Analysis

1. Make sure all parameters match the default values above. If they do not, click on the "Reset" button.

    a. The distribution center is currently located closest to Retailers 3 and 5, and is farthest from Retailers 1 and 4. Explain why this has occurred.

    b. Move Retailer 4 thirty miles directly south, from (80,50) to (80,20). How much did the optimal location of the distribution center move?

2. Set the parameters back to their starting defaults.

    a. Record the location of the distribution center. Move Retailer 2 thirty miles directly north, from (64, 65) to (64, 95). How much did the optimal location of the distribution center move?

    b. Explain why the results of moving Retailer 4 thirty miles was different from the results of moving Retailer 2 thirty miles.

3. Set the parameters back to their default values.

    a. Currently, Retailer 1 requires four times as many shipments as Retailer 3. Move Retailer 1 forty miles to the east, from (20, 20) to (60, 20). What is the impact on the optimal location of the distribution center? What are its new coordinates? How far did it move?

b. Set the parameters back to their defaults. Move Retailer 3 forty miles to the east, from (50, 40) to (90, 40). What is the impact on the optimal location of the distribution center? What are its new coordinates? How far did it move?

c. Move Retailer 4 forty miles to the south, from (80, 50) to (80,10). What is the impact on the optimal distribution center location?

d. Move D2 forty miles to the south, from (64, 65) to (64, 25). What is the impact on the distribution center location?

e. Based on the four previous experiments, what is the relationship between quantity of shipments and the effect of the destination location on the optimal distribution center location?

Process Simulation Models

Models in This Unit:

The Waiting Line Simulation Model

The Production Line Simulation Model

The Kanban Simulation Model

The Constraint Management Simulation Model

Unit 7 provides four process simulation models. Process simulation models are capable of showing a functioning system over time and allow users to watch as the system functions. Parameters that affect system performance can be changed, and the results can be monitored and measured. The first model in this unit, the **Waiting Line Simulation Model,** provides a queuing simulation with flexibility for the user to modify the number of servers, the number of phases, the arrival rate, and the service rate.

The remaining four models offer various modifications of production line simulations. The **Production Line Simulation Model** is a general-purpose simulation for examining production line dynamics and the effects of process time variability and disruptions. The **Kanban Simulation Model** provides a typical Kanban system with the flexibility to change Kanban policies and experiment with varying levels of process variability. The final simulation, the **Constraint Management Simulation Model,** expands the production line simulation model to allow the user to incorporate buffers to protect a constraint from upstream disruptions.

The Waiting Line Simulation Model

The Waiting Line Simulation Model provides a rich environment for exploring service systems. The user can select between 1- and 2-phase systems. The simulator speed allows the user to slow the system down to better observe interactions. The arrival rate is generated from a Poisson distribution with parameter λ that is the number of arrivals per hour. The service rate (parameter μ) is generated from a negative exponential distribution and is the number of customers served per hour. The selection of NS1: or NS2: determines the number of servers for each phase of the system. Output measures are:

- W_q = the average time customers wait in line
- W_s = the average time customers spend in the system (waiting and being served)
- L_q = the average number of customer waiting in line for the service
- L_s = the average number of customers in the system (waiting and being served)

Exhibit 7.1 shows the Waiting Line Simulation Model.

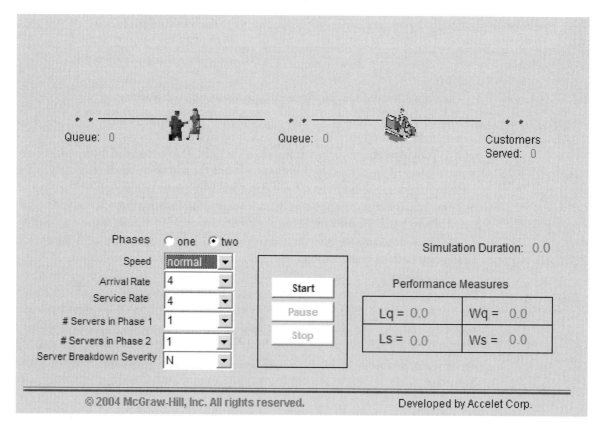

EXHIBIT 7.1   Screen View of the Waiting Line Simulation Model

Interactive Case

Managing Lines at the Passport Office

The Dane County Administration Office processes passport applications as a part of its service. The office has recently received a small grant to spend to improve the passport application process. As a means of stretching the money as far as possible, Sandy Harris has incorporated the use of an operations management class as consultants. Currently the process can be described as a single server, 2-phase queuing system with an average service rate of 4 customers per hour and an average arrival rate of 4 customers per hour. Sandy wishes to have a complete analysis done and wants the student team to demonstrate how queues work and explain to her how the various queue characteristics interact.

Check to see that the parameters are equal to the values below.

Phases	2
Speed	Normal
Arrival Rate	4
Service Rate	4
# Servers in Phase 1	1
# Servers in Phase 2	1
Server Breakdown Severity	N

Analysis

1. Run the simulation, observing the system, until 50 customers have been served.

   a. Were both servers ever busy at the same time? Did a waiting line ever form in front of either server? What was the maximum length of the waiting lines? What were the output measures for W_q, W_s, L_q, and L_s? Explain each.

2. Run the simulation with the same parameters except increase the number of servers for each phase from 1 to 2.

   a. Did waiting lines ever form this time? How long did they get? What were the new output measures for W_q, W_s, L_q, and L_s? Explain the difference.

   b. Why would lines form, given the service capacity at each server and the arrival rate?

3. Run the simulation with the same parameters (2 servers at each phase), but change the server breakdown severity to "Y." Run the simulation for 50 customers.

   a. Did waiting lines form? If so, how long did the lines get? What were the new output measures for W_q, W_s, L_q, and L_s?

b. Explain the changes. What happened to the performance measures as breakdowns became a factor? Is this what you expected to happen?

4. Reset the parameters as follows. Note that this configuration uses 2 employees, as was the case in the original configuration, but each employee performs the entire service, rather than splitting it between 2 workers in 2 phases. Since each worker does the entire service, each server can only process 2 customers per hour. Total capacity, however, is still 4 customers per hour.

Phases	1
Speed	Normal
Arrival Rate	4
Service Rate	2
# Servers in Phase 1	2
# Servers in Phase 2	0
Server Breakdown Severity	N

a. Carefully observe the simulation as it processes 50 customers. How long does the queue in front of the first server get? With arrival rate and server rates equal, why does a queue develop? Did you notice any instances of the second server being idle (yellow, rather than blue)? Why did this happen? After 50 customers, what were the output measures for W_q, W_s, L_q, and L_s?

b. Leave all parameters the same as in 4a, except change the service rate to 4. Again, observe the simulation as it processes 50 customers. How long does the queue in front of the first server get this time? Did you notice any instances of either server being idle? Why did this happen? After 50 customers, what were the output measures for W_q, W_s, L_q, and L_s? Compare them to the output measures for 2a. Explain how the differences relate to the change in service rate.

Most fast-food restaurants, banks, and airline ticket counters have adopted a single queue, multiple-server design that utilizes a long "serpentine" queue. The customer at the head of the line goes to the first open server. These systems are fair in that no one gains advantage by selecting the line with the fastest server. It also eliminates the problem of customers jumping from one line to another (jockeying).

5. Set the parameters as follows:

Phases	1
Speed	Slow
Arrival Rate	8
Service Rate	2
# Servers in Phase 1	4
# Servers in Phase 2	0
Server Breakdown Severity	N

a. What are the performance measures? Do you think they're acceptable? What would you expect to be true about the utilization of the servers? Would that performance measure be important?

6. Reset the parameters as follows:

Phases	1
Speed	Slow
Arrival Rate	8
Service Rate	3
# Servers in Phase 1	4
# Servers in Phase 2	0
Server Breakdown Severity	N

a. How would you judge the performance of this configuration from the standpoint of waiting time and line length, as well as resource utilization?

7. Based on the parameters and simulations you have run, provide a general description of the relationship between the number of servers, service rate, arrival rate, and the performance measures.

The Production Line Simulation Model

The Production Line Interactive Model provides an environment designed for exploration of processes and the roles disruptions can play in those processes. In the Production Line Interactive Model, the user can specify the input rate and the production rate for each of five work centers. In addition, the user can specify the level of variability in the process as well as the frequency of breakdowns. The user has four controls of the simulation itself. The first control is the start button. Starting the simulation causes the work centers to begin processing. The second control is of the clock speed. Speeding up the lock simply means that the simulation runs faster. The pause button allows the user to temporarily suspend the simulation. The stop button ends the simulation.

Exhibit 7.2 shows the Production Line Simulation Model.

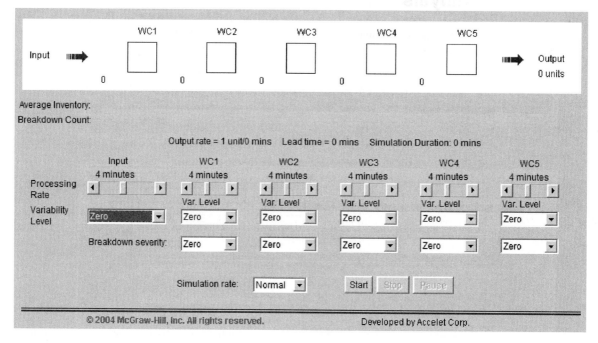

EXHIBIT 7.2   Screen View of the Production Line Simulation Model

The default values are a 4-minute input rate, a 4-minute processing rate for all five work centers, zero variability, and zero breakdown severity for the input and all five work centers.

Interactive Case

Process Improvement for CaseWorks Systems

CaseWorks Systems is a contract assembler of automotive parts. They specialize in short assembly processes of high-volume components. One particular assembly line consists of automatic machines, each with an operator. These five machines (WC1, WC2, WC3, WC4, and WC5) perform a variety of operations that are standard to many of the components assembled by CaseWorks Systems. The variety of components that use the line, however, result in processing times that vary from job to job, and in some cases, process times that are difficult to control. Changes in processing times, as well as variability in the system, have made it difficult for managers to predict process outputs and, to be frank, have them quite confused.

Analysis

1. Set the input rate and processing time for all WCs at 4 minutes per unit with zero variability. Run the simulation for 100 simulator minutes.

   a. How many units were complete?

   b. Why weren't 25 units completed?

2. Set WC3 to a 6-minute processing time. Leave the variability at zero for all WCs. Run the simulation for 100 simulator minutes.

   a. How many units were complete this time?

   b. What happens in front of WC3?

   c. Repeat the 100-minute simulation with WC3 processing at 6 minutes per unit, but reduce the input rate to one unit every 6 minutes. Now what happens?

3. Set the processing time of all WCs and the input rate to 6 minutes with zero variability. Run the simulation for 100 simulator minutes.

   a. How many units were complete?

   b. What factors determine the number of units completed by the system in a set amount of time?

4. Set the input rate and processing time for all WCs back to 4 minutes per unit, with zero variability. Run the simulation for 100 simulator minutes.

   a. How many units were complete?

5. Reduce the processing time of any one of the five WCs to 3 minutes. Run the simulation for 100 simulator minutes.

   a. How many units were complete?

6. Reduce the processing time of an additional WC to 3 minutes. Run the simulation for 100 simulator minutes.

   a. How many units were complete?

   b. Why did a reduction in time not result in an improvement in system output?

   c. What does this tell you about investing in equipment to improve the speed of operations in service and manufacturing systems?

7. Set all processing times and the input rate to the initial 4-minute value with zero variability. Run the simulation for 100 simulator minutes.

   a. Examine the use of resources during this time. Does inventory build up anywhere? Where?

   b. Are any of the work centers idle (white) during this time?

8. Leave the input rate and processing times at 4 minutes, but increase the variability of WC3 to the extreme level. Run the simulation for another 100 simulator minutes in five separate runs, recording the number of units produced for each simulation run.

   a. What is the average output?

   b. Observe the simulation runs. Does inventory build up anywhere? If so, where does it build up? Explain why this happens.

   c. After the initial startup phase, are any of the WCs ever idle? If so, which ones? Explain your observations.

   d. What implications does process time variability have for the productivity of resources?

9. Leave the input rate and processing times at 4 minutes, but increase the variability of all WCs and the input rate to the extreme level. Run the simulation five separate times for 100 simulator minutes each time. Record the results.

   a. What is the average output? How does this outcome differ from the previous five simulation runs?

   b. Does inventory build up anywhere? If so, where does it build up? Explain why this happens.

   c. After the initial startup phase, are any of the WCs ever idle? If so, which ones? Explain the results.

   d. The average processing time for each WC is the same in the last two experiments. What is happening to make system output different? What implications does this have for the productivity of resources in a process?

The Kanban Simulation Model

The Kanban Simulation Model provides an interactive simulation of a kanban system. For each work center in the model, the user can set the processing rate by adjusting the corresponding sliding bar, the variability in the processing rate, and the breakdown severity. In addition, the user can set the maximum buffer size that precedes each work center. Work centers are only authorized to produce when the feeding inventory buffer is below its maximum. All work centers have the same maximum buffer size. When the simulation is paused or stopped, the average inventory for each work center and total number of breakdowns for each work center are provided. The user can also select the simulation speed from three options: slow, normal, and fast.

Exhibit 7.3 shows the Kanban Simulation Model.

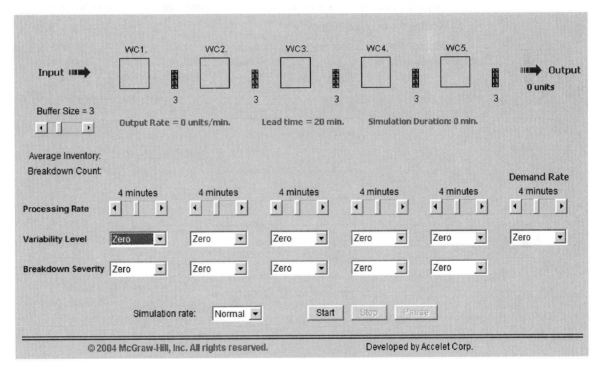

EXHIBIT 7.3   Screen View of the Kanban Simulation Model

Interactive Case

Implementing Kanban at Simmon's Electric

Simmon's Electric produces electronic controls for a variety of customers, including automotive manufacturers, heating and air conditioning equipment manufacturers, and the defense industry. One high-volume production line rotates its production among several different control models. That production line consists of five work centers, with visible buffers of inventory between the work centers and after the final work center.

Analysis

1. Check the default parameters to make sure your system starts with these values:

Buffer size	3
Processing Times	
Work center 1	4
Work center 2	4
Work center 3	4
Work center 4	4
Work center 5	4
Demand rate	4
Variability	
Work center 1	Zero
Work center 2	Zero
Work center 3	Zero
Work center 4	Zero
Work center 5	Zero
Breakdown Severity	
Work center 1	Zero
Work center 2	Zero
Work center 3	Zero
Work center 4	Zero
Work center 5	Zero
Simulation rate	Slow

    a. Start the simulation. In your own words, describe what is happening.

2. Stop the simulation and set the demand rate to 1 unit every 6 minutes. Leave the processing times at 4 minutes for all work centers. Leave the process time variability and breakdown severity at zero. Start the simulation. Whenever a work center box is gray, it means that it is idle.

   a. Are work centers ever idle? Why?

   b. Using the pause button, pause the simulation while work centers are idle. Explain the different possible causes for a work center to be idle.

3. Reset all settings back to the default values, except WC3. Set the processing time of WC3 to 1 minute.

   a. How does the system function differently than when all parameters were at the default?

   b. What is happening at WC3 and at the inventory buffer immediately after WC3?

4. Set the parameters as shown below.

Buffer size	3
Processing Times	
Work center 1	4
Work center 2	8
Work center 3	4
Work center 4	8
Work center 5	4
Demand rate	4
Variability	
Work center 1	Zero
Work center 2	Zero
Work center 3	Zero
Work center 4	Zero
Work center 5	Zero
Breakdown Severity	
Work center 1	Zero
Work center 2	Zero
Work center 3	Zero
Work center 4	Zero
Work center 5	Zero
Simulation rate	Normal

a. Start the simulation and let it run for 100 simulation minutes. Observe what happens to the use of the work centers and inventory buffers as it runs. What is the system output after 100 minutes? Stop the simulation.

b. Leave the parameters as they are, with the exception of the maximum buffer size. Change it from 3 to 2 units. Run the simulation for 100 simulator minutes. Does the system appear to behave any differently? What is the output?

c. Leave everything the same except reduce the maximum buffer size to 1. Run the simulation again for 100 simulator minutes. Observe what happens. What is the output in 100 minutes? Explain what happens.

d. Based on the previous three simulation runs, what does the buffer do to aid in the utilization of work centers? Is it needed?

5. Set the parameters as below:

Buffer size	1
Processing Times	
Work center 1	4
Work center 2	8
Work center 3	4
Work center 4	8
Work center 5	4
Demand rate	4
Variability	
Work center 1	Zero
Work center 2	Zero
Work center 3	Extreme
Work center 4	Zero
Work center 5	Zero
Breakdown Severity	
Work center 1	Zero
Work center 2	Zero
Work center 3	Severe
Work center 4	Zero
Work center 5	Zero
Simulation rate	Normal

a. Run the simulation for 100 simulator minutes. What is the output? What do you observe to be the effect of the variability at work center 3?

b. Leave the parameters as is, with the exception of work center 5. Increase its variability to "extreme" and its breakdown severity to "severe." Run the simulation for 100 simulator minutes. What is the output? What was the impact of having high variability on WC3 and WC5?

c. Now add extreme levels of variability and severe levels of breakdown severity to all work centers. Run the simulation for 100 simulator minutes. What is the new level of output?

d. With the variability and breakdown at maximum levels, incrementally increase the maximum size of the buffer by one unit for each simulation run. What happens? Explain the relationship between variability and disruptions, inventory buffer size, and system productivity.

The Constraint Management Simulation Model

The Constraint Management Simulation Model provides an interactive environment for experimenting with system parameters and various combinations of constraint buffers to aid in the exploitation of system constraints. The input rate and processing times at each of the five work centers can be varied from 1 to 8 minutes per unit. The variability of each can be controlled as well, from zero to extreme. In addition to the variability, breakdowns can be from zero to severe. The user can create buffers in front of any work center by establish the beginning level of inventory, ranging from zero to 5 units. In addition to the quantity of products produced by the system, utilization on each work center is provided when the system is stopped. The user also has the option to set the simulator clock speed and can pause the simulation.

Exhibit 7.4 shows the Constraint Management Simulation.

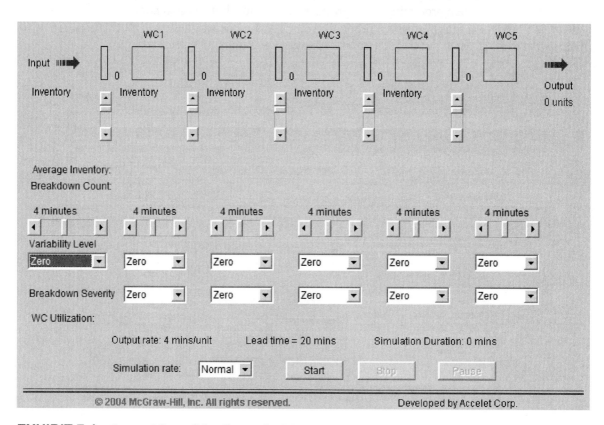

EXHIBIT 7.4   Screen View of the Constraint Management Simulation

Interactive Case

Understanding Production Output at Henckley's Outdoor Products

Henckley's Outdoor Products manufactures a variety of products for outdoor recreational use, but focuses primarily on canvas products such as awnings, tents, and canopies, as well as the poles and hardware used with them. One particular production line produces aluminum extension poles for large awnings that are used primarily for large outdoor receptions and parties. That line is a short, five-station line that cuts, drills appropriate holes, and assembles various poles for the awning. Adam Henckley, the owner of the company, has had trouble getting consistent output from the line, despite the amount of work that has gone into its design. For one particular pole, the one the line was designed around, the average processing time for each step is 4 minutes. Adam has seen productivity fluctuate when producing other products on the line, but has also noticed inconsistencies in output even when producing the pole the line was designed to produce. Adam has also noticed that, at times, work-in-process inventory levels between some of the work centers are high.

Analysis

1. Set the parameters to the default values, as shown below.

	Initial Inventory	Processing Time	Variability	Breakdown Severity
Input	0	4	Zero	Zero
WC1	0	4	Zero	Zero
WC2	0	4	Zero	Zero
WC3	0	4	Zero	Zero
WC4	0	4	Zero	Zero
WC5	0	4	Zero	Zero

a. Run the simulation for 100 simulator minutes. How many products are completed?

b. Increase the processing time for WC3 from 4 to 5 minutes and run the simulation again for 100 minutes. What happens to the number of products finished? What happens to the level of inventory in the system? What happens to the utilization of each work center?

    c. Change the input rate to 1 unit every 5 minutes, (leaving WC3 at 5 minutes also). What happens now? What does that indicate about the role of the constraint and the system input rate? How do utilization rates change for each work center?

2. Set the parameters back to the original default values.

    a. Increase the processing time variability for WC3 to the extreme level. Run the simulation for 100 simulator minutes. What is the finished product output? How does this compare to the results from 1a? What happens to inventory in the system? How does process time variability affect inventory levels at the various work centers? How are work center utilizations affected?

    b. Increase the variability of WC3 even more by changing the breakdown severity to "extreme." Run the simulation for 100 simulator minutes. What is the new finished product output? How does this compare to the results from 2a? What happens to inventory in the system? How are the work centers affected by increased variability? How are work center utilizations affected by this change?

3. Set the parameters to the values shown below.

	Initial Inventory	Processing Time	Variability	Breakdown Severity
Input	0	6	Zero	Zero
WC1	0	4	Zero	Zero
WC2	0	4	Zero	Zero
WC3	0	6	Zero	Zero
WC4	0	4	Zero	Zero
WC5	0	4	Zero	Zero

    a. Run the simulation for 100 simulator minutes. How many products are finished?

4. Set the parameters to the values shown below.

	Initial Inventory	Processing Time	Variability	Breakdown Severity
Input	3	6	Zero	Zero
WC1	3	4	Extreme	Severe
WC2	3	4	Extreme	Severe
WC3	3	6	Zero	Zero
WC4	3	4	Zero	Zero
WC5	3	4	Zero	Zero

a. Run the simulation for 100 simulator minutes. How many products are finished? Do you notice as much idle time on WC3? What is the utilization of WC3?

5. Reset the parameters as shown below.

	Initial Inventory	Processing Time	Variability	Breakdown Severity
Input	0	6	Zero	Zero
WC1	0	4	Extreme	Severe
WC2	0	4	Extreme	Severe
WC3	2	6	Zero	Zero
WC4	0	4	Zero	Zero
WC5	0	4	Zero	Zero

a. Run the simulation for 100 simulator minutes and observe what happens. How many products are finished? Does a buffer of 2 units prior to WC3 effectively isolate it from disruptions? Do you notice any idle time on WC3? What is the utilization of WC3?

6. Reset the parameters as shown below.

	Initial Inventory	Processing Time	Variability	Breakdown Severity
Input	0	6	Zero	Zero
WC1	0	4	Extreme	Severe
WC2	0	4	Extreme	Severe
WC3	4	6	Zero	Zero
WC4	0	4	Zero	Zero
WC5	0	4	Zero	Zero

a. Run the simulation for 100 simulator minutes. How many products are finished?

b. Does a buffer of 4 units prior to WC3 effectively isolate it from disruptions? Do you notice idle time on WC3? What is the new utilization of WC3?

7. Set the parameters to the values shown below.

	Initial Inventory	Processing Time	Variability	Breakdown Severity
Input	0	4	Extreme	Zero
WC1	0	4	Extreme	Severe
WC2	0	6	Zero	Zero
WC3	0	4	Zero	Zero
WC4	0	4	Zero	Zero
WC5	0	4	Zero	Zero

  a. Run the simulation for 100 simulator minutes. How many products were complete?

  b. How does that compare to the same configuration with zero variability and zero breakdowns for all work centers? Would you conclude that the difference is due to processing variability and disruptions?

8. Set the parameters to the values shown below.

	Initial Inventory	Processing Time	Variability	Breakdown Severity
Input	0	4	Extreme	Severe
WC1	0	4	Extreme	Severe
WC2	0	4	Extreme	Severe
WC3	0	6	Zero	Zero
WC4	0	4	Zero	Zero
WC5	0	4	Zero	Zero

  a. Run the simulation 100 simulation minutes. How many units are produced?

9. Set the parameters to the values shown below.

	Initial Inventory	Processing Time	Variability	Breakdown Severity
Input	0	4	Extreme	Severe
WC1	0	4	Extreme	Severe
WC2	0	4	Extreme	Severe
WC3	0	4	Extreme	Severe
WC4	0	6	Zero	Zero
WC5	0	4	Zero	Zero

a. Run the simulation for 100 simulator minutes. What happens?

b. Is the effect of these changes caused by increased variability? Or by moving the constraint? How could you find out for sure? Perform the necessary experiments to confirm your hypothesis.